COMINCH P-0012

I0203761

AMPHIBIOUS OPERATIONS

CAPTURE OF IWO JIMA

16 FEBRUARY TO 16 MARCH 1945

UNITED STATES FLEET

Headquarters of the Commander in Chief

Published by Books Express Publishing
Copyright © Books Express, 2011
ISBN 978-1-78039-504-3

Books Express publications are available from all good retail and online booksellers. For
publishing proposals and direct ordering please contact us at: info@books-express.com

REQUEST FOR/OR NOTIFICATION OF REGRADING ACTION

For use of this form, see AR 380-5; the proponent agency is OACSI.

DATE	24 April 1987
FILE	FILE

READ INSTRUCTIONS ON REVERSE SIDE BEFORE COMPLETING THIS FORM

TO: *(Include ZIP Code)*
Chief of Naval Operations
09N Navy Dept (Mr. Bob Allen)
The Pentagon
Washington, D.C. 20350-2000

FROM: *(Include ZIP Code)*
Commandant
USACGSC
ATTN: ATZL-SWS-L (MAIL)
Fort Leavenworth, KS 66027-6900

☐ THE DOCUMENT(S) DESCRIBED BELOW HAS/HAVE BEEN REVIEWED FOR REGRADING AND ACTION HAS BEEN TAKEN AS INDICATED. APPROPRIATE ACTION SHOULD BE TAKEN TO MARK YOUR COPIES AND NOTIFY ALL RECIPIENTS TO WHOM ADDITIONAL DISTRIBUTION WAS FURNISHED IN ACCORDANCE WITH AR 380-5. DOCUMENTS CONCERNING THIS SAME SUBJECT SHOULD BE REVIEWED FOR POSSIBLE REGRADING.

☒ REQUEST DOCUMENT(S) DESCRIBED BELOW BE REVIEWED TO DETERMINE WHETHER THEY CAN BE DOWNGRADED OR DECLASSIFIED AT THIS TIME. *(Include justification in the "REMARKS" section of this form.)*

☐ REQUEST APPROPRIATE CLASSIFICATION/REGRADING INSTRUCTIONS FOR DOCUMENTS DESCRIBED BELOW.

CONTROL NUMBER	DESCRIPTION *(TYPE, FILE REFERENCE, UNCLASSIFIED SUBJECT OR SHORT TITLE, INDORSEMENTS, INCLOSURES)*	CLASSIFICATION/ REGRADING INSTRUCTIONS	
		OLD	NEW
C-16564.50	Document, SUBJ: Xerox Copy, Short Title, AOCOIJ 16F16M45 (U). COMINCH P-0012. United States Fleet Headquarters of the Commander in Chief. NOTE: Request OPSEC Review for public domain. If document cannot be declassified request appropriate Title classification.	CONF	

PRINTED OR TYPED NAME AND TITLE OF OFFICER	SIGNATURE
BERTINA BYERS C, Information Services Combined Arms Research Library	*Bertina Byers*

DA FORM **1575**
1 SEP 77

EDITION OF 1 SEP 62 IS OBSOLETE.

IN REPLY REFER TO

5531/6
NSIC-211B3/424

From: Commander, Naval Security and Investigative Command
To: Commandant, USACGSC, Attn: ATZL-SWS-L (mail)
       Fort Leavenworth, KS 66027-6900

Subj: REQUEST FOR DECLASSIFICATION REVIEW

Ref: (a) DA Form 1575 of 24 April 87

Encl: (1) Short Title, AOCOIJ16F16M45, COMINCH P-0012, United
           States Fleet Headquarters of the Commander-In-Chief

1. Security policy matters addressed to the Chief of Naval
Operations are acted upon by Commander, Naval Security and
Investigative Command.

2. In reply to reference (a), enclosure (1) has been reviewed
and declassified and determined suitable for public release.

                        M.F. Brown
                        R. R. GORENA
                        By direction

UNITED STATES FLEET
HEADQUARTERS OF THE COMMANDER IN CHIEF
NAVY DEPARTMENT
WASHINGTON 25, D. C.

17 JULY 1945.

This publication "Amphibious Operations—Capture of Iwo Jima—16 February to 16 March 1945" continues the series promulgating timely information drawn from action reports. It follows "Amphibious Operations—Invasion of the Philippines, CominCh P–008."

Material contained herein has not been subjected to exhaustive study and analysis, but is issued in this form to make comments, recommendations, and expressions of opinion concerning war experiences readily available to officers engaged or interested in amphibious operations. It should be widely circulated among commissioned personnel.

This publication is classified as secret, nonregistered. It shall be handled as prescribed by Article 76, U. S. Navy Regulations 1920. When no longer required it shall be destroyed by burning. No report of destruction need be submitted.

This publication is under the cognizance of, and is distributed by the Commander in Chief, United States Fleet.

Transmission by Registered Guard Mail or U. S. registered mail is authorized in accordance with Article 76 (15) (e) and (f), U. S. Navy Regulations.

B. H. BIERI,
Acting Chief of Staff.

DISTRIBUTION LIST FOR COMINCH P–0012

STANDARD NAVY DISTRIBUTION LIST NO. 29, 15 JUNE 1945

List 1   a (1) less Cominch; ComPac (5), ComThird (3), ComFifth (3); b (1); c (1); less ComFairShip-Lant, ComFairShipPac, ComGenAirFleetMarForce, DirAviation, MC; d (1); e (1); g-ComPhibPac (5), ComPhibPacAdmin (5), ComThirdPhib (3), ComFifthPhib (1), ComPhibGroups (2), ComLandCraftFlot (1), PhibTra7thPhib (2), 7thPhibAdmin (1), Com7thPhib (3), ComPhibTraPac (35); h (1) less ServLantSubCom; i (1) less ComSec #115, #117, ComNorthCalifSecWesSeaFron, ComNorWesSecWesSeaFron, ComSouthCalifSecWesSeaFron; j (1); k only to COTCLant (1), COTCPac (3), ComFltTraCom, 7thFlt (1), PreComTraCenCOTC-Pac (6), ComSanDiego, San Pedro Shakedown Group (1); 1-only to Chief of Staff to Commander in Chief, Army & Navy (1).

List 2   a–3 (1); a–10 FairWings only (1); a–18 only to Fleet Aircraft Recog Unit (1); a–19 only to ComUtWingServ (1); f (1); g (1); n (1) less LCT Groups; o (1) MinRons only; v (1).

List 3   b (1); c (1); d (1); f (1); m (1); p (1); t (1); u (1); v (1); x (1); kk (1); oo (1); rr (1); vv (1); zz (1); www (1); ffff (1); gggg (1); jjjj (1).

List B–3   Construction Brigades and 36th Constr. Regiment only (1).

STANDARD NAVY DISTRIBUTION LIST NO. 32, 1 JUNE 1945

List 6   a (1) less SevRivNavCom, Comdt PotRivNavCom, SamDefGrp; b only to CNAOpTra Jacksonville, Fla. (25), CNATra Pensacola, Fla. (1).

List 7   a–1 (1) less NYdNavy #128; d–1 (1) only to NAB's 1st to 13th ND incl., and NavAirTrBases, Corpus Christi and Pensacola; e (1); f (5); g (30); h (5); i–3 (2) only to Newport, R. I.

List 11   SecNav (1); UnderSecNav (1); AsstSecNav (1); AsstSecNavAir (1); ChrmGenBd. (2); InspGen (1); BuAero (5); BuPers (10); CNO (1); BuOrd (5); BuShips (5); BuY&D (5); USMC (900); USCG (3).

List 14   q (2).

Plus Special Distribution.

Numbers in parentheses indicate number of copies sent to each addressee.

CONTENTS

Chapter VII.   MISCELLANEOUS—Continued.

LIST OF EFFECTIVE PAGES

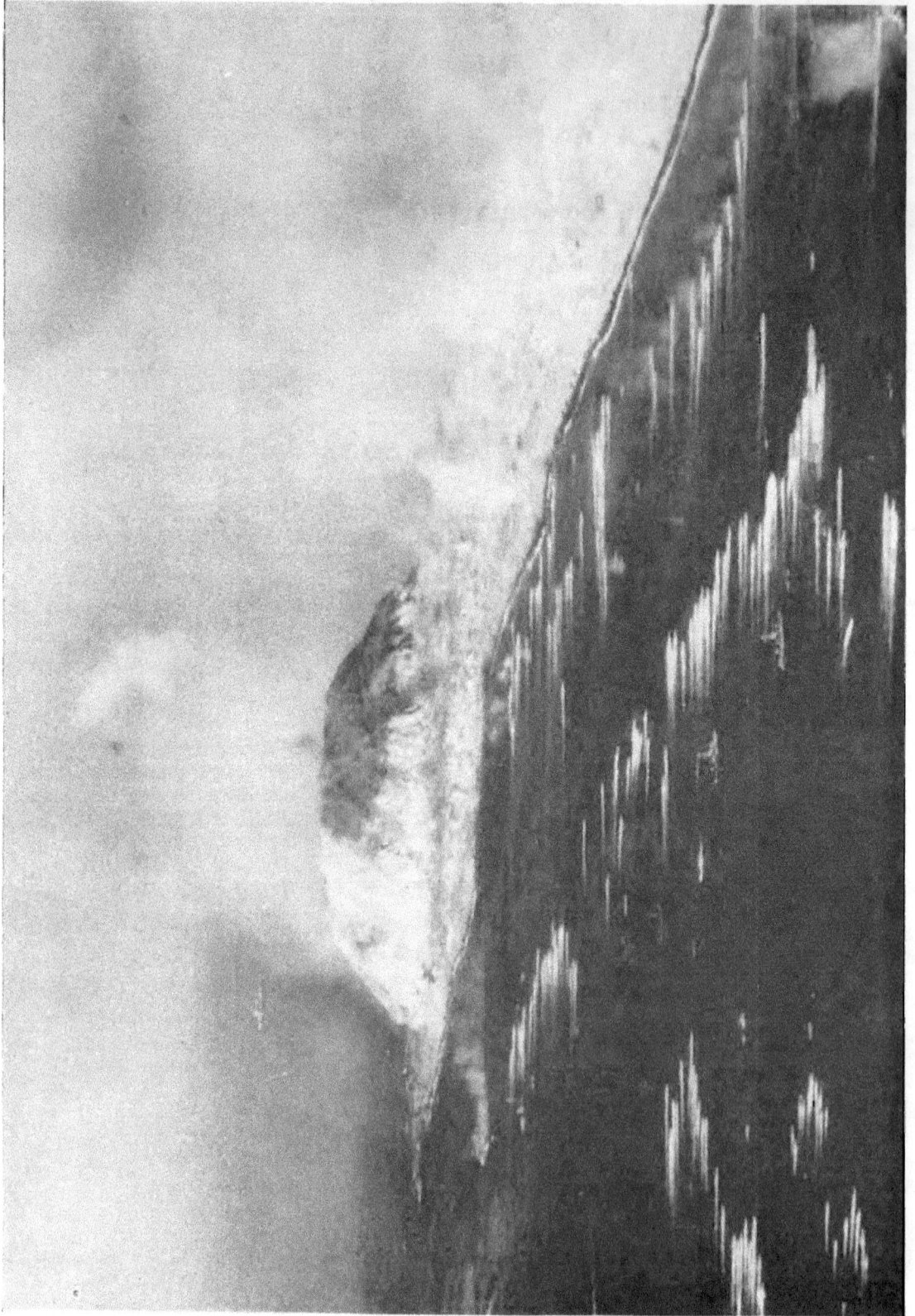

Invasion Showing Initial Waves Moving Into Southeastern Landing Beaches, First, Second, Third Waves, D-Day (H-Hour-Minus-1).

Chapter I. NARRATIVE

From: ***Commander Fifth Fleet***

The capture and occupation of the Marianas Islands gave our forces bases from which targets in the Japanese Empire could be subjected to VIR air attacks. In order to operate with greatest effectiveness and with a minimum of attrition, fighter cover for the long range bombers was required at the earliest practicable time. Iwo Jima was admirably situated as a fighter base for supporting long-range bombers between the Marianas and the Empire and offered sites for three airfields. Accordingly the Commander in Chief, Pacific Ocean areas, issued his Operation Plan No. 11–44, directing the Commander Fifth Fleet, as Commander Central Pacific Task Forces, to capture, occupy, and defend Iwo Jima and develop air bases on that island, to reduce Japanese naval and air strength and production facilities in the Japanese homeland, and to protect air and sea communications along the Central Pacific axis.

The planning for and the actual execution of the Iwo Jima operation were affected to a considerable extent by the operations in the Philippines which immediately preceded it, and by the necessity of preparing for the Okinawa operation which was to follow it.

The Philippine operations necessitated last minute changes and reduced the total number of ships which had been previously allocated to the Iwo Jima operation. This applied primarily to battleships, cruisers, and destroyers for the Joint Expeditionary Force, although other forces were also affected to a lesser extent. The only source from which additional gunfire support ships could be obtained was from Task Force 58 (Fast Carrier Force). In order to provide the necessary additional battleships for gunfire support, the Commander in Chief, United States Pacific Fleet, authorized the use of the *North Carolina* and *Washington* for this purpose. These two ships were, accordingly, loaded principally with bombardment ammunition, their service allowance of armor piercing ammunition being correspondingly reduced. Certain cruisers of Task Force 58 were also loaded with some additional bombardment ammunition.

The Okinawa operation affected the Iwo Jima operation in two ways. First, it was felt that the threat of Japanese land based aircraft, while taking Okinawa, would be very great, both because of the great value of that island to us when we took it and because of its closeness to the Empire (325 miles). Therefore, anything which we could do during the Iwo Jima operation to reduce Japanese air strength, either in aircraft and, even more, in aircraft production facilities, would help the Okinawa operation as well as support the Iwo Jima operation. The second way in which the Okinawa operation and the Iwo Jima operation affected each other was in the close timing of the two operations. D-day for the Iwo Jima operation was 19 February. L-day for the Okinawa operation had been set as 1 April. If the fighting ashore on Iwo Jima were prolonged, it might be difficult to carry out the plans for the Okinawa operation which called for initial carrier operations to start off Kyushu on L-minus-14 (18 March) and off Okinawa on L-minus-9 (23 March).

Commander Fifth Fleet's Operation Plan No. 13–44 was issued on 31 December 1944. Principal commanders were assigned as follows:

> Commander Joint Expeditionary Force (TF 51)— Vice Admiral R. K. Turner.
> Commander Fast Carrier Force (TF 58)—Vice Admiral M. A. Mitscher.
> Commander Expeditionary Troops (TF 56)—Lt. Gen. H. M. Smith, U. S. M. C.
> Commander Amphibious Support Force (TF 52)— Rear Admiral W. H. P. Blandy.
> Commander Attack Force (TF 53)—Rear Admiral H. W. Hill.
> Commander Logistic Support Group (TG 50.8)— Rear Admiral D. B. Beary.
> Commander Search and Reconnaissance Group (TG 50.5)—Commodore D. Ketcham.
> Commander Service Squadron 10 (TG 50.9)—Commodore W. R. Carter.

The general plan of the operation was as follows: Commence operation on D-minus-3-day (16 February), with a simultaneous fast carrier strike on the Tokyo area and bombardment of Iwo Jima by the Amphibious Support Force.

Fast carrier operations were planned to carry out a 2- to 3-day strike on the Tokyo area, the

By this time the decision had been reached that the situation at Iwo Jima was such that Task Force 58, less Task Group 58.5, could be released from its support of the Iwo Jima operation, in order to prepare for the Okinawa operation. One task group proceeded direct to Ulithi, while the remaining three, after refueling, made a strike on Okinawa on 1 March, the primary purpose of which was to obtain additional photographs required for the Okinawa operation. On conclusion of this successful 1-day strike, these three task groups proceeded to Ulithi, where preparations were made for the coming Okinawa operation.

The withdrawal of four of the five task groups of Task Force 58 left available for air support at Iwo Jima the CVE's of Task Group 52.2 and Task Group 58.5. These ships were also required for the Okinawa operation. The date of their release depended upon the activation of an airfield on Iwo Jima and the establishment on it of sufficient day and night fighters to protect the area from Japanese air attacks, to furnish the air support required by the troops who were still fighting on the island, and to keep out of use the enemy airfield on Chichi Jima. The progress of the fighting on Iwo Jima posed a similar problem as affecting the release of the ships of the Joint Expeditionary Force which were furnishing support for the troops ashore. Fortunately, all forces were released in time to make the necessary preparations required for the Okinawa operation, although in the case of Task Group 58.5 only 2 days at Ulithi were available, which permitted no time for upkeep.

In addition to the air support furnished by Task Force 58 and the CVE's of Task Group 52.2, the patrol planes of Fleet Air Wing One (TG 50.5) conducted searches by PB4Y's based on Tinian, to cover the areas between Iwo Jima and Japan. When the airfield on Iwo was ready, certain of these search sectors were extended by having the PB4Y's in those sectors stage through Iwo for additional gasoline on their return legs. Before this field was ready for use, patrol plane tenders anchored in the lee of Iwo Jima to service PBM's of Task Group 50.5 at such times as sea conditions would permit the operation of seaplanes. These PBM's were used for dumbo missions and for the extension of the more important search sectors toward Japan, commencing on 28 February. The tenders and PBM's were withdrawn when activation of the airfield ashore permitted their replacement by land planes and amphibians. The performance of the PBM's, with jet assisted take-off, in the bad sea conditions which normally existed around Iwo Jima, was a remarkable tribute to the ability of their pilots.

Enemy reaction to the Iwo Jima operation was very strong against the landings and the succeeding troop operations on shore. In spite of ample naval gunfire and air support, it was not until 16 March, after 26 days of hard fighting with heavy casualties, that all organized resistance ceased. The normal tactics evolved from previous Pacific operations were used and were proved to be sound against the strongest defense system the enemy was capable of erecting. It should be noted that these tactics were employed with skill and resolution by veteran troops. In view of the character of the defenses and the stubborn resistance encountered, it is fortunate that less seasoned or less resolute troops were not committed. The Fifth Amphibious Corps with its component Third, Fourth, and Fifth Marine Divisions added many new pages to the records of heroic achievements in battle of the officers and men of the United States Marine Corps.

The enemy's air reaction to the Iwo Jima operation was not strong. No damage was inflicted on Task Force 58 while it was making the two strikes on the Tokyo area and the photographic strike on Okinawa. In the vicinity of Iwo Jima, however, a Japanese air attack of an estimated 50 planes arrived about dusk on the evening of 21 February and inflicted considerable damage. The *Saratoga* was hit by 4 suicide planes, which caused fires and extensive damage but did not affect the mobility of the ship. She proceeded to Pearl Harbor via Eniwetok. The *Bismarck Sea* (CVE) was hit on the stern by a suicide plane. As a result of fires and explosions that followed, she capsized and sank with heavy casualties. The *Lunga Point* (CVE), *Keokuk*, and LST *477* also suffered minor damage in this attack.

Enemy surface force reaction to the operation was lacking.

The Logistic Support Force, organized under a flag officer with the *Detroit* as his flagship, was given a trial and work-out during the Iwo Jima operation. The function of this force was to permit ships of the Fleet—particularly those of the carrier task forces—to remain at sea over long periods by supplying underway as many of their logistic needs as possible. The real need for this was to come during the Okinawa operation, when the distances from rear bases were greater, the distance from the objective to Japan was less, the operation was expected to last longer, and the carrier task force had to remain at sea in support over a much longer period. To the services rendered during earlier operations by the fleet oilers and the transport CVE's there was added ammunition replenishment by ammunition ships. In addition, provisions were given to smaller types, critical items of supplies were brought out, and mail service was improved.

From: *Commander Task Force 58 (Commander First Carrier Task Force)*

This action report is submitted in broad form to provide a framework into which the more detailed reports of the task group commanders, ships' commanding officers and air groups may be fitted. The task force organization included 11 CV's, 5 CVL's, 8 BB's, 1 CB, 5 CA's, 11 CL's, 81 DD's, and over 1,200 airplanes.

During the period from 16 February to 1 March inclusive, planes from Task Force 58 flew a total of 5,514 sorties over the target including 185 dawn, dusk and night combat air patrol and night VT observer sorties over Iwo Jima. In addition a very large number of day combat air patrol, antisnooper patrol, search and other miscellaneous sorties were flown. During these operations aircraft from the Task Force actually dropped or launched at their targets 1,118.65 tons of bombs, 218 napalm bombs, 12 torpedoes, and 9,896 rockets. In addition, during the Toyko strikes destroyers sank several enemy fishing and picket boats by gunfire. Cruisers and destroyers of the Force conducted a night bombardment of Okino Daito Island starting steady fires, and destroyers conducted a night bombardment of Parece Vela rocks with unobserved results. Battleships, cruisers, and destroyers on detached duty from the force engaged in fire support missions at Iwo Jima.

Aircraft losses in combat from 16 February to 1 March inclusive were 46 F6F, 1 F6F (N), 21 F4U, 1 F4U (P), 3 SB2C, 12 TBM, or a total of 84 aircraft of all types. Operational losses during the

days of offensive air operations were 24 F6F, 7 F6F (N), 8 F4U, 4 SB2C, 13 TBM, 3 TBM (N) or a total of 59 aircraft of all types. Two of the VTN lost operationally were shot down by antiaircraft fire from friendly forces near Iwo Jima in bad weather during a daylight air raid alert.

During the same period, combat losses of flight personnel were 60 pilots and 21 aircrewmen. Operational losses were 8 pilots and 6 aircrewmen. In addition to rescuing personnel from the Force, destroyers assisted by planes rescued 8 survivors from a ditched B-29.

From: *Commander Amphibious Forces, United States Pacific Fleet (Commander Joint Expeditionary Force)*

The Joint Expeditionary Force (Task Force 51), a part of the Fifth Fleet, commenced active preparation for the operation in accordance with the provisions of CinCPOA Top Secret Dispatch, serial 092200 as of 9 October 1944, at which time certain units were made available to Commander Amphibious Forces, United States Pacific Fleet for planning and training.

The Joint Expeditionary Force, Task Force 51, as of target date, was composed of the following principal components:

(a) *Amphibious Support Force* (Task Force 52), Rear Admiral W. H. B. Blandy, U. S. N., commanding, comprising an air support control unit, support carrier group, mine group (Rear Admiral Sharp, U. S. N., commanding), underwater demolitions group, gunboat support group, mortar support group, and an RCM rocket support group, with the mission of pre-Dog-Day gunfire and air support, minesweeping, mooring buoy and net laying, beach reconnaissance and underwater demolitions.

(b) *Attack Force* (Task Force 53), Rear Admiral H. W. Hill, U. S. N., commanding and second in command of the Joint Expeditionary Force, comprising an air support control unit, two transport squadrons, tractor groups, LSM groups; control group, beach party group, and a pontoon barge, causeway and LCT group, with the mission of transporting and landing the expeditionary troops.

(c) *Gunfire and Covering Force* (Task Force 54), Rear Admiral B. J. Rodgers, U. S. N., commanding, comprising three battleship divisions, one cruiser division, three destroyer divisions, augmented on Dog-Day with two destroyer divisions from Task Force 58, and on Dog-plus-One-Day by two cruiser divisions and two destroyer divisions from Task Force 58, with the mission of shore bombardment, and cover in the vicinity of the objective against enemy surface attack.

(d) *Expeditionary Troops* (Task Force 56), Lt. Gen. H. M. Smith, U. S. M. C., commanding, and consisting of all assault troops, plus certain assigned garrison troops, with the mission of executing the ground attack for the capture, occupation, and subsequent defense of the objective. Included was the *Landing Force* (Task Group 56.1), Maj. Gen. H. Schmidt, U. S. M. C., commanding, comprising the assault troops (Task Group 56.2), consisting of the V Amphibious Corps (4th MarDiv, Maj. Gen. C. B. Cates, U. S. M. C., commanding, and 5th MarDiv, Maj. Gen. K. E. Rockey, U. S. M. C., commanding), plus attached units; garrison force (Task Group 10.16), commanded by Maj. Gen. J. E. Chaney, A. U. S. comprising units of the Army Air Force, Antiaircraft Artillery, Coast Artillery, with service and other units assigned; expeditionary troops reserve (Task Group 56.3), Maj. Gen. G. B. Erskine, U. S. M. C., commanding, and comprising the Third Marine Division, plus attached units.

(e) *Air Support Control Unit* (Task Group 51.10), Capt. R. H. Whitehead, U. S. N., commanding, with the mission of support aircraft control, and air-sea rescue operations.

(f) *Joint expeditionary Force Reserve* (Task Group 51.1), Commodore D. W. Loomis, U. S. N., commanding, consisting of one transport squadron, with the mission of transporting and landing the Expeditionary Troops Reserve when required.

(g) *Transport Screen* (Task Group 51.2), Captain Moosbrugger, U. S. N., commanding, comprising two destroyer squadrons and all escort vessels available at the objective and not employed for fire support and escort duty.

(h) *Service and Salvage Group* (Task Group 51.3), Captain Curtiss, commanding.

(i) *Hydrographic Survey Group* (Task Group 51.4), Commander Sanders, commanding.

(j) *Defense and Garrison Groups* (Task Groups 51.5, 51.6, 51.7, 51.8, and 51.9), comprising the first echelons of the Garrison Forces for Iwo Jima. Succeeding Garrison echelons, embarked by authorities other than CTF 51, assembled at Eniwetok and proceeded to the objective as ordered. On arrival, these elements operated under the Senior Officer Present Afloat, but were not integral parts of Task Force 51.

Summary of ships employed.—A total of 495 ships classified as to type in the table below were attached to, and employed by Task Force 51 during this operation. The list includes assault shipping and that of the Zero and First Garrison Echelons but does not include ships from other forces which operated temporarily under the Senior Officers Present Afloat, Iwo Jima.

Summary of ships employed

Type	Number	Type	Number	Type	Number	Type	Number
AGC	4	ATF	2	DD	44	OBB	6
AK	2	ATR	2	DE	38	PC	7
AKA	16	AV	1	DM	8	PCE	1
AKN	2	AVD	2	DMS	6	PCE(R)	1
AM	16	AVP	1	LCI	58	PCS	10
AN	5	BB	2	LCS(L)	12	SC	12
AP	1	CA	9	LCS(L)3	6	YMS	13
APA	43	CB	1	XAP	3		
APD	6	XAK	7	LCT	12	Total ships	495
ARB	1	CL	9	LSD	3		
ARG	1	CM	1	LSM	31		
ARL	1	CV	1	LSV	1		
ARS	3	CVE	11	LST	63		

Summary of expeditionary troops engaged.—A statistical record of troops engaged in the operation appears in the table below. Navy personnel figures include only personnel assigned to duty ashore, including LCT and pontoon barge and causeway crews, boat pools, and Beach parties.

Summary of Expeditionary troops employed

	Assault troops		Garrison troops			Total
	Army	Marine	Army	Marine	Navy	
Landing force	570	70,647			3,927	75,144
Garrison force			23,830	492	11,842	36,164
Net total troops employed	570	70,647	23,830	492	15,769	111,308

In furtherance of the general objective of the United States Pacific Fleet in the Western Pacific, the Joint Expeditionary Force (Amphibious Forces, U. S. Pacific Fleet) was, as a part of the Fifth Fleet, assigned the mission for the capture, occupation and defense of Iwo Jima. The Fifth Fleet covered the amphibious part of the operation by attacks on Japan and local cover, and directly supported it with aircraft and gunfire bombardment in support of troops, and by providing night fighter cover. The Fifth Fleet was assisted by other forces under the control of the Commander in Chief, Pacific Ocean area, the Commander Southwest Pacific area, and the Twentieth Bomber Command. The strategy employed in this operation included these salient points:

(a) Bases in the Hawaiian Islands and the Marianas served to lift and mount the Expeditionary Force.

(b) Bases in the Marshalls and Marianas functioned as regulating stations, provided the protection for sea and air lines of communication, and facilities for staging.

(c) Bases in the Marianas enabled the assembly of the combined Task Force prior to its final movement to the objective.

(d) The Amphibious Support Force and Gunfire and Covering Force struck Iwo Jima for 3 days prior to Dog-Day with naval gunfire and air bombardment in order to soften up the enemy defenses, destroy his fortifications, destroy his aircraft, and to neutralize his airfields.

(e) The Fast Carrier Force struck the Tokyo area and the Nagoya-Kobe area simultaneously with the pre-Dog Day bombardment of Iwo Jima by our surface vessels for the purpose of destroying enemy aircraft and air facilities which might interfere with the Iwo Jima operation. Later this force furnished air cover and direct support at Iwo Jima.

(f) Shore-based aircraft operating in the Central Pacific, Southwest Pacific, and from bases in China and India, supported the operation through air reconnaissance, antisubmarine searches, offensive screens, air-sea rescue missions, and photo reconnaissance.

(g) The Strategic Air Force, Pacific Ocean areas, operating land aircraft from bases in the Marianas, struck military installations in the Nanpo-Shoto for a period of several months prior to Dog-Day with heavy concentrations on Iwo Jima and Chichi Jima for the purpose of softening up enemy defenses, destroying his aircraft and shipping, and neutralizing his airfields. It further furnished photo reconnaissance of the Nanpo-Shoto and engaged in air and sea rescue.

(h) The Twentieth Air Force employed the Twentieth Bomber Command by strikes on Kyushu both preliminary to and simultaneously with the carrier strikes on the Tokyo area. The Twenty-first Bomber Command increased its bombing tempo in the Tokyo area prior to the carrier strikes, coordinated its strikes with those of the carrier groups and covered the carrier retirement by strikes in the Tokyo area.

(i) The Amphibious Support Force and Gunfire and Covering Force supported the Landing Force with reinforcing fires and air bombardment on the beaches, and with deep supporting fires inland during the assault and occupation phase of the Operation.

(j) The Submarine Force, Pacific Fleet, provided intelligence relative to movements of enemy Naval Units, through reconnaissance off enemy bases and routes of approach, and attacks on enemy shipping. It also engaged in lifeguard service, accomplished photo missions, and furnished weather reports.

(k) The Marianas and Hawaiian bases provided a means for the rehabilitation of the assault troops following their evacuation from the objective.

The Amphibious Support Force (TF 52) and the Gunfire and Covering Force (TF 54) arrived at the objective at Dog-minus-Three-Day. From this time until Dog-Day minesweeping of all mineable waters was completed; and a reconnaissance of both the preferred and alternate landing beaches was conducted by the underwater demolition teams. TF 54 delivered destructive fires against selected enemy positions, engaged in counterbattery fire, and covered the minesweeping and UDT operations.

The Attack Force (TF 53) arrived in the transport areas off the eastern beaches prior to daylight on Dog-Day 19 February and took position for debarking the Landing Force (TG 56.1). At 0600 (K) Dog-Day; the Amphibious Support Force (TF 52) passed to direct command of CTF 51, who then also assumed the title of CTF 52. Following intensive air and naval bombardments, the Fourth and Fifth Marine divisions landed on Iwo Jima at How-Hour, 0900 (K), as scheduled. The initial boat waves met only slight opposition. Later in the day, however, the beach areas were subjected to heavy enemy artillery and mortar fire. Some fire was directed into the beach approaches and the LST Areas, registering a few hits. The natural features of terrain plus an exploitation of camouflage rendered almost perfect concealment to enemy gun emplacements. Many could not be located, and our troops and boats had to "stand and take it."

On Dog-Day air strength was concentrated for the Pre-How-Hour and How-Hour strikes. Aircraft were supplied by the CVE's of Task Group 52.2 augmented by planes from Fast Carrier Task Groups 58.2, 58.3, and 58.5. A small force of Army B24's was scheduled to assist but arrived late and could be used only in part. The large number of carrier planes was organized to create the maximum destructive effect with bombardment at How-minus-50-minutes. They then harassed and neutralized exposed enemy gunners at How-Hour in order to protect the final movement of the assault waves to the beach.

The adverse beach conditions soon became apparent. With a steep gradient such as this, the surf breaks directly upon the beach. It was impossible with the heavy swells to prevent the landing craft from broaching. With each wave, boats were picked up bodily and thrown broadside to the beach where succeeding waves swamped and wrecked them. Losses had to be accepted until the beachhead was secured, and until LST's, LSM's and LCT's could be employed. The resultant accumulation of wreckage piled progressively higher, and extended seaward into the beach approaches to form underwater obstacles which damaged propellers and even gutted a few of the landing ships.

Although from seaward the beach appeared hard-packed, it was soon discovered that volcanic ash has no cohesive consistency. Wheeled vehicles bogged to their frames. A few tanks bogged in the surf and were swamped. Even tracked vehicles moved with difficulty. The first terrace has a 40 percent grade which proved insurmountable for some amphibious tractors. This was the problem that faced the boat crews and troops, and despite it the attack moved forward. A trail of wreckage marked the way.

LST's and LSM's were sent to the beaches as soon as the beachhead was secured. These, too, had difficulty to keep from broaching. Several failed when anchors did not hold. Tugs were in constant attendance to tow them clear. Unloading continued day and night with the beach parties working "around the clock." Ships of the

Gunfire and Covering Force delivered call fire missions during the day and starshell illumination and harassing fires throughout the night. As ammunition ran low in the destroyers of TF 54, rotation was made with destroyers of the screen. The Gunboat Support Groups were stationed close to shore in sectors around the northern end of the island and delivered night harassing and destructive fires (including mortars and rockets) against enemy positions. Their presence also deterred the enemy from shore to shore overwater movements. The gunboats were regularly taken under fire by enemy guns. None was hit, and destroyers which supported them were enabled to silence some of the enemy batteries.

Difficulties of unloading and replenishment persisted—not only on the beaches but also in the transports. The weather closed down at 1500 (K), Dog-plus-One-Day, with strong winds and heavy swells curtailing air operations. Throughout this period unloading and replenishment had to be carried out underway. This was difficult for unloading since the distance to the beach and the urgent need for speed had constantly to be borne in mind. Restricted movement resulted in many operational casualties to the ships—which of necessity had to be accepted.

To alleviate the surf problem on the beaches, and to permit continued employment of boats, it was decided to launch the pontoon causeways as soon as practicable. However, they could not be employed successfully. All attempts to anchor the seaward ends of the barges were unsuccessful. Like the boats, they also broached, were damaged and sank, or ran adrift; and in every status became a menace to navigation. Decision was then made to launch the LCT's; to employ these craft plus LSM's and LST's only for unloading; and to close the beaches to craft smaller than LST's. The only exception was the employment of amphibious vehicles, which worked very successfully, for the evacuation of casualties.

Vessels not engaged in unloading retired each night and returned to the transport area after daylight. Task groups not scheduled to unload remained in operating areas, usually to the southeast, until ordered forward. The limited size of the objective area and the large number of ships involved required careful scheduling of times of arrival, and demanded arrival after, rather than at, daybreak.

The necessary dense concentration of the assault shipping in the comparatively narrow area off the assault beaches is probably partially responsible for the large number of collisions which occurred in this operation. The beaches were narrow by reason of the physical characteristics of the island. The number of troops carried involved a large amount of shipping. Sea conditions made boating difficult, and it was imperative that the distance to the beaches be kept at a minimum. In addition the gunnery problem demanded that certain fire support ships position themselves along the edges of the transport area in order to properly deliver the fire required. This added to the congestion. Other causes of collisions were inexperienced personnel and unfavorable weather.

Collisions occurred between landing craft and landing ships, between landing ships and gunboats, between fire support ships and transports, and between ships of the same types. These are explained in detail in another section of this report.

The UDT's and beach parties cleared the beaches of accumulated wreckage. The Service and Salvage Group cleared the beach approaches, salvaged boats and pontoons, and effected emergency repairs to damaged ships. These were herculean tasks and proceeded apace with the unloading, the replenishment, the evacuation of casualties, and the rendering of supporting fires so that the assault might continue.

Throughout the operation aircraft were maintained on station for direct support missions on targets requested by the troops or as indicated desirable by air observation or photographic intelligence. Air Spot for naval gunfire was provided by cruiser and battleship seaplanes and by fighters from a special spotting squadron based in Wake Island. Tactical observers were maintained in the air continuously, aerial photographers were flown and propaganda leaflets were dropped. Combat air patrol was maintained over Iwo on a 24-hour-a-day basis with special emphasis on the dawn and dusk periods. Continuous day and night air antisubmarine protection was given to the objective by carrier TBM planes.

The largest and most destructive enemy air attack was made by an estimated 50 Betty's and Zeke's, which attacked carriers and amphibious ships at Iwo from 1640 to 2000 on Dog-plus-Two (21 February). Enemy planes were divided into small groups for their attacks. *Saratoga, Bismarck Sea, Lunga Point, Keokuk,* and LST 477 were hit by suiciders. *Saratoga* suffered three hits by suicide planes on the intial attack and one hit on attacks slightly later. She was badly damaged and forced to return for navy yard repairs. Her losses were 25 dead, 57 wounded. *Bismarck Sea* was struck by a suicide plane aft. The intial explosion was followed by fire and later by explosions of her torpedoes which caused her to sink, 100 officers and 513 men surviving the sinking out of a total complement of 124 officers and 836 men. One enemy plane was shot down by *Saratoga* fighter and 15 by antiaircraft fire from ships. Of the 15 *Saratoga* planes which were airborne when she was hit, 5 landed safely on her, 4 landed on CVE's, 4 landed in the water but pilots were rescued, and only 2 are missing. All *Bismarck Sea* planes were on board at the time of sinking and were lost.

The fast carriers less *Enterprise* departed on Dog-plus-three for their second strike on Tokyo. Thereafter all air activities were furnished by the CVE's plus *Enterprise*, with two minor exceptions: On 25 and 27 February nine Army B24's made a bombing attack on Northern Iwo. *Enterprise* furnished dusk and night fighters, neutralized Chichi and Haha Jima with dawn and dusk sweeps and made searches. The CVE's provided all direct support for the troops, the day CAP, day and night ASP, plus special flights.

To augment the Fourth and Fifth Marine Divisions, two RCT's of the Third Marine Division (RCT 21 and 9) were landed on Dog-plus-Two and-Five respectively. The commanding general, Third Marine Division was assigned a zone of action in the center of the line between the Fourth and Fifth Marine Divisions.

During this period Dog-plus-One to Dog-plus-Five an unprecedented number of call fire missions were delivered. This was due to the restrictive effect of the weather upon air support, and to the enemy's strong resistance. Replenishment and unloading were slow. Whereas the slowdown in unloading permitted the beach parties to improve beach conditions, the ammunition situation both afloat and ashore became critical. On Dog-plus-Four it was difficult to find ships with sufficient ammunition to deliver the call fires requested. Fortunately on the night of Dog-plus-Four the weather cleared, and Dog-plus-Five found wind and sea greatly moderated with visibility and ceiling unlimited. Marked progress in the beach clearance program was now evident, and unloading and ammunition replenishment were accelerated.

Special seaplane service for the purpose of carrying urgent news matter to CinCPac Guam commenced Dog-Day, and, except when prevented by bad weather, was continued throughout the operation until the captured airfield on Iwo was made serviceable. Although seaplane tenders arrived on Dog-plus-One-Day enemy activity in the vicinity of Mount Suribachi prevented the establishment of the seaplane base off the southeastern shore until Dog-plus-Five-Day. Seaplane mooring buoys were laid and the tenders moved to inshore anchorages. The first search seaplanes were delayed in arriving from Saipan until Dog-plus-Eight due to bad weather. Searches were commenced the following day. A total of 15 search PBM's and 3 dumbo PB2Y Seacats were operated from the seaplane base. All were equipped with jet-assisted take-off devices to enable them to get off rough water more rapidly and with a greater load. On Dog-plus-Fifteen (6 March) PB4Y search planes commenced employing the airfield on Iwo as a staging base to increase their radius from Tinian to 1,200 miles. At this time seaplane activities were curtailed and the search seaplanes returned to Saipan. On 8 March 3 PBY5A Landcats arrived at Iwo and took over dumbo operations. The dumbo seaplanes then returned to Saipan as did the tenders. The seaplane base was decommissioned on 8 March.

On Dog-plus-Five (24 February) the Hydrographic Survey Group (TG 51.4) completed a survey for locating mooring buoys and nets. Since Dog-Day it had been noted that, regardless of weather, so long as easterly winds prevailed the resultant swell continued to make conditions difficult on the eastern beaches. The front lines had advanced sufficiently to indicate the feasibility of a shift to the western beaches. Consequently, on Dog-plus-Six, a survey of Purple and Brown beaches was commenced. It was found that these beaches would be excellent for boats, but that the water was too shallow for craft larger than an LSM. The situation indicated that these beaches could best be used initially for unloading ammunition; and plans for creating exits ashore from these beaches proceeded accordingly. On Dog-plus-Ten (1 March) *Columbia Victory* proceeded to take station for unloading off the western beaches. No sooner did she approach this area than she was taken under fire by enemy coast defense guns in the northwestern end of the island. After having been straddled several times, and having received superficial damage with one man wounded from flying fragments, she withdrew. Unloading to the western beaches was therefore postponed one day until the enemy guns could be silenced. Off the northern end of the island *Terry* and *Colhoun* were hit by enemy coast defense guns on 1 March. These guns also were silenced.

The first United States aircraft to commence operations from Iwo were OY–1 artillery spotting planes on 27 February. Twenty OY aircraft were brought to Iwo, 2 each in 7 CVE's and 6 in LST *776* which is equipped with the Brodie device. Two were lost in the sinking of *Bismarck Sea* and 1 was lost in launching from the Brodie LST. The remaining 17 were in operation from Iwo by 1 March, and flew both day and night missions spotting for artillery.

Air delivery of supplies by parachute was made from three Saipan-based R5C's on 28 February. The next day mail for the troops on shore was dropped by parachute from an R5C airplane. Parachute delivery continued until transport planes commenced operations at the field on 2 March. Air supply and air evacuation were conducted on a large scale from then on.

On 3 March the situation from a naval standpoint became relatively quiet, and continued so throughout the remainder of the operation. Good weather had remained at the objective since 24 February. The enemy had been forced into the narrow northern sectors of the island. Although enemy artillery, mortar and some rocket fire continued to land in the beach areas, this fire was sporadic and registered few hits. Unloading and evacuation progressed favorably over both eastern and western beaches and by 3 March all the assault shipping including the Defense Group (TG 51.5) and the Joint Expeditionary Force Reserve (TG 51.1) had been unloaded and retired to rear areas. Garrison Group Zero (TG 51.6) arrived in the transport areas on 2 March and commenced unloading. Garrison Group One (TG 51.7) was en route.

On 4 March *Sumner* (AGS 5) and YP 42 arrived to commence a general hydrographic survey of Iwo Jima. Meanwhile the operation for laying the antisubmarine nets was suspended. Volcanic ash apparently covers the ocean's bottom throughout this area, forming such poor holding ground as to create doubt that the net buoy anchors would hold. A further survey was indicated, and the net officer of CTF 94 was called forward for consultation. As a result of further survey, it was determined that the net-laying plan was feasible; and the operation was commenced on 11 March.

As soon as garrison aircraft could be accommodated at south field Iwo they flew in from Saipan. The first were Army P51 day fighters and P61 night fighters which arrived on 6 March, and took over local day and night CAP. Two days later more P51's and a squadron of VMTB arrived. The VMTB commenced flying day and night ASP on 10 March. By 11 March all air activity at Iwo was provided by shore-based aircraft operating from the captured field.

By 7 March enemy-occupied territory had become so restricted that naval gunfire support could be provided only to a very limited extent. Therefore the major portion of TF 54 was ordered to Ulithi for upkeep. ComCruDiv 5 in *Salt Lake City* with *Tuscaloosa* and destroyers present remained as Gunfire and Covering Force until 12 March when they also retired to Ulithi. Carriers departed from Iwo for Ulithi in three groups. On 8 March *Makin Island*, *Lunga Point*, *Rudyerd Bay*, *Natoma Bay*, and *Petrof Bay* departed. On 9 March *Enterprise* departed. On 11 March the remaining CVE's departed from Iwo Jima and all carrier support was withdrawn.

On 9 March Commander Joint Expeditionary Force (CTF 51) ordered TF 51 dissolved, and turned over command of the operation to CTF 53 who thereafter assumed title CTG 51.21 as Sopa Iwo Jima. The Commander Landing Force (CTG 56.1) thereafter assumed title CTG 51.27, while the island commander retained his designation CTG 10.16.

Throughout the operation, commencing Dog-plus-One (20 February) hospital ships *Samaritan* and *Solace* made shuttle trips between Iwo Jima and Saipan or Guam for the evacuation of serious

personnel casualties. These trips were augmented by employment of *Pinckney* (APH 2) and *Bountiful*, with one round trip each. In addition four hospital LST's (LST(H) 929, 930, 931, 1033) were in position off the assault beaches for the immediate reception of casualties from Dog-Day through Dog-plus-Nine-Day (28 February). These LST(H)'s acted as "Field Hospitals", and after necessary surgery and treatment, casualties were transferred to retiring transports. The more serious cases were transferred to the hospital ships for further treatment. Air evacuation was inaugurated after 2 March when the airfield was opened to transport planes.

Numerous submarine contacts with several sightings were made during this operation. In every case hunter-killer groups were ordered to the point of contact and persistent search maintained, until positive evaluation could be made. Evidence indicates that several "kills" were obtained.

On 8 March the wind shifted into the northwest and caused heavy swells on the western beaches. Unloading in this area was interrupted, and ships moved to the eastern side of the island. Garrison Group One arrived and commenced unloading. The next day Garrison Group Zero completed unloading and retired to rear areas. By 14 March Garrison Group One had completed unloading, and Garrison Group Two had arrived to commence unloading. Meanwhile the net laying operation, which was initiated on 11 March, proceeded favorably and on 19 March 4,000 feet of net had been installed. Unloading over both eastern and western beaches continued intermittently, dependent upon the weather and surf conditions, throughout the remainder of the operation.

The assault continued favorably, registering only small daily gains, as the enemy became more and more compressed into the northern portion of the island. Naval gunfire support was limited to destroyer call fires and night harassing assignments. By 13 March enemy artillery and mortar fire had ceased, and resistance resolved into small arms and hand-to-hand fighting.

The airfields on Iwo Jima commenced "paying dividends" soon after being placed in operation. In addition to providing safe landings for many carrier planes in difficulty, the South field proved a haven to many B-29's. On 17 March 16 B-29's returning from a strike against the Empire utilized Iwo for emergency landings. Two days later six of this type aircraft landed for refueling or repairs. Central airfield was placed in operation on 16 March.

It has been noted that enemy picket boats stationed in the approach areas to the Empire were providing advance warning of impending strikes against Japan. TF 58, in its strikes against Tokyo during this operation, had destroyed several of these picket boats. B-29's reported sighting several on patrol north of Chichi Jima. Sopa Iwo Jima (CTG 51.21) therefore, on 13 March, formed TU 51.24.1 composed of *Dortch* and *Cotten*, and ordered a surface sweep of the area between latitude 30–00 N. and 31–00 N. and longitude 144–00 E. and 145–00 E. to be made during 14 and 15 March. One enemy vessel, identified as *Yatsue O Maru* or *Fiji Maru* was contacted during this search and destroyed.

The National Ensign was raised officially on Iwo Jima at 0930 (K) 14 March 1945. All organized resistance was declared as having ceased at 1800 (K) 16 March. The Fourth Marine Division commenced reembarkation the following day, with the Fifth Division the day after. Division headquarters were closed on Iwo Jima on 19 March and 20 March respectively, and on 20 March the Fourth Marine Division departed for Maui for rehabilitation. On 20 March the Garrison Force (147th Inf. Div.) arrived at Iwo Jima. Meanwhile combat requirements in the "mopping up" operation delayed reembarkation of the Fifth MarDiv until 25 March by which time all enemy pockets of resistance were eliminated. The Third MarDiv also continued "mopping up" operations. On 26 March Iwo Jima was turned over to the Island Commander and the Commander Forward Area. The Fifth MarDiv and Corps Troops completed reembarkation on 28 March and departed for rehabilitation in the Hawaiian area. The following day the Third MarDiv departed for rehabilitation at Guam.

FROM D-MINUS-3 (16 FEBRUARY) TO D-DAY (19 FEBRUARY)

From: Commander Amphibious Group ONE, Commander Amphibious Support Force

The function of this command during subject period was to exercise general supervision over, and coordinate, all activities at the objective prior to the arrival of the landing and assault elements of the Joint Expeditionary Force on Dog-Day (19 February). The forces participating in these prelanding activities of Task Force 52 were:

(*a*) The Gunfire and Covering Force, Task Force 54, under command of Rear Admiral B. J. Rodgers, U. S. N. (Commander Amphibious Group Eleven), consisting of 6 OBB's, 4 CA's, 1 CL, 15 DD's, 1 DM, and 1 AVD.

(*b*) The Support Carrier Group, Task Group 52.2, under command of Rear Admiral C. T. Durgin, U. S. N. (Commander Escort Carriers, U. S. Pacific Fleet), consisting of 8 CVE's, 5 DD's, and 9 DE's.

(*c*) The Mine Group, Task Group 52.3, under command of Rear Admiral A. Sharp, U. S. N. (Commander Minecraft, U. S. Pacific Fleet), consisting of 7 Sweep Units comprising 43 minecraft plus 8 LCP(R)'s rigged for shallow water minesweeping.

(*d*) The Underwater Demolition Group, Task Group 52.4, under command of Capt. B. H Hanlon, U. S. N. (Commander Underwater Demolition Teams, U. S. Pacific Fleet), consisting of 6 APD's carrying UDT's Nos. 12, 13, 14, 15.

(*e*) Gunboat Support Units One and Two, Task Units 52.5.1 and 52.5.2, under command of Commander M. J. Malanaphy, U. S. N. (Commander LCI Flotilla Three), consisting of 1 LCI(L) and 12 LCI(G)'s.

(*f*) Land-based heavy bombers of the Strategic Air Force, Pacific Ocean Areas, Task Force 93, delivered air strikes under the control of Commander Air Support Control Unit, Task Group 52.10, Capt. E. C. Parker, U. S. N., embarked in the flagship of Commander Task Force 52, when weather permitted.

The mission of forces under this command was to effect the maximum possible destruction of enemy forces and defenses of Iwo Jima by aircraft and surface ship bombardment, minesweeping, and underwater demolition, during the period D-minus-3 to D-minus-1, inclusive, in order to facilitate its capture.

The general plan of operations at Iwo Jima for 16 February consisted, briefly, of sweeping adjacent waters to within approximately 6,000 yards of the shore, gunfire at long (above 12,000 yards) and medium (from 6,000 to 12,000 yards) ranges with air spot for destruction of defenses and silencing of enemy batteries, air strikes by support carrier aircraft and land-based heavy bombers of TF93, examination of beaches from the air by special hydrographic observers, aircraft photo missions in late morning and afternoon, installation of a navigational light on Higashi Iwa, a small rocky islet about 3,000 yards to the eastward of Iwo Jima, and early morning and late afternoon fighter sweeps against Chichi Jima to destroy planes and ships or boats which might interfere with the operation. Fire support ships were to follow minesweeping units in toward the island and then work in their assigned sectors inside a screen of destroyers and APD's which enclosed the island area. APD's were to conduct visual reconnaissance of beaches, but not to approach closer than 3,000 yards. This plan was followed, except that low ceiling and intermittent showers prevented the photo mission, the morning strike against Chichi Jima, the strike of land-based bombers, and severely handicapped the spotting planes. CTF 52, in order to prevent waste of ammunition, directed ships to fire only when efficient air spot was available. It was not possible to follow the planned firing schedules, and instead each ship fired in its assigned area of responsibility whenever weather permitted. Two enemy luggers were discovered early in the morning by support aircraft about 30 miles west of Suribachi Mountain. They were attacked and left burning and in a sinking condition, with crews abandoning ship. In the early afternoon a *Pensacola* spotting plane reported shooting down a Zeke which had apparently taken off from Iwo Jima. Three Betty's were strafed and probably destroyed on the ground. A battery which opened fire on minesweepers from northern flank of eastern beach was quickly silenced by fire support ships. None of our ships was hit. One fighter plane and pilot became lost in thick weather and did not return. One plane was an operational loss. One fighter plane was shot down by enemy AA but the pilot was recovered uninjured. One *New York* spotting plane was damaged on catapulting, and sank after personnel were removed. Results of minesweeping were negative, but one old mine adrift was sighted and sunk. Excellent reports were received from the air hydrographic observer indicating that beaches and surf conditions would permit landings by any type of landing craft. He could see no evidence of underwater defenses. Lack of photographs and the paucity of observed results by ships and aircraft prevented accurate assessment of damage to enemy installations. It was estimated, however, that the comparatively small amount of firing permitted by the intermittent thick weather had inflicted little damage on major defenses. Pilots reported enemy heavy AA gunfire not particularly intense or effective, and fire of Automatic AA intense but generally inaccurate.

At sunset all ships commenced night deployment away from the island, except for four destroyers which were designated to remain and provide harassing fire and illumination, interdict the use and repair of airfields, and prevent escape or reinforcement of the garrison. CTF 52 in *Estes*, screened by 4 AM's, after following the fire support units away from the island during dusk, returned to the vicinity of the island to supervise night operations.

Operations planned for 17 February consisted in general of morning and evening fighter sweeps against Chichi Jima; close range destructive fire against eastern beach defenses during which minesweeping up to about 150 yards from the eastern shore would be covered by the heavy ships; UDT reconnaissance of eastern beaches in the late morning closely supported by heavy ships, 7 destroyers and 7 LCI(G)'s; strikes by land-based bombers at 1330; close range destructive fire on western beaches; minesweeping off western beaches and UDT reconnaissance of these beaches supported as in the morning; minesweeping to within about 2,000 yards of the northern and northeastern shore; hydrographic observation of beach conditions from the air, photo missions, and night operations at the objective as on 16 February. At 0124 (K) ComDesDiv 111 in *Newcomb*, with *Halligan*, was directed to proceed to point (Lat. 26° 00' N, Long. 141° 50' E.) and to act as radar pickets and provide life guard services for air strikes against Chichi Jima. At 0641 (K) *Halligan* was attacked by three Betty's when 24 miles, bearing 355°, from Suribachi Mountain. She drove off the attackers, shooting down one Betty. Fire support ships arrived on station and commenced the scheduled bombardment promptly at 0700 (K). Mine Unit Two, in company with Gunboat Support Units One and Two, arrived at 0700 (K). Gunboat support units reported to

CTG 52.4 and Sweep Units 5 and 6 to CTG 52.3. A special air strike group of 12 VF's departed for Chichi Jima at 0735 (K). The first support air strike group reported on station at 0715 (K). During the day many air strikes were launched against the objective through meager to intense heavy and light antiaircraft fire. Photographic missions were completed, but the morning verticals were poor, preventing accurate damage assessment. The fire support ships were ordered to close the eastern beaches at 0803 (K) for close destructive bombardment. Under cover of this fire, and supported by two destroyers, Sweep Units 5 and 6 proceeded with operations along the eastern shore. APD's with UDT's embarked, destroyers and LCI(G)'s began assembling off the eastern beaches about 0930 for execution of the UDT reconnaissance. At 0938 the *Pensacola*, off the northeastern shore, was observed to be under fire by apparently quite heavy caliber guns as some splashes appeared to be almost as high as her foremast. She sustained extensive damage and many casualties. A plane was set on fire. The ship continued to fire as she withdrew to extinguish the fires and repair damage. She continued to carry out her mission, ceasing fire from time to time while casualties were being operated on and given blood transfusions. CTG 52.3 requested additional support for Sweep Unit 4 working off the northeastern shore, and *Vicksburg* was ordered to provide it. By 1048 (K) all units were in position to commence the UDT reconnaissance set for 1100 (K). The last of the minesweepers was completing the sweep off the eastern beaches, these small ships having gallantly passed close along the eastern shore in precise formation, firing as they went, without deviation from their prescribed tracks although under occasional enemy fire. The UDT reconnaissance commenced exactly on schedule. As the LCI(G)'s moved in toward the beach, enemy fire began to concentrate on them. By 1105 (K), when they reached a point 1,000 yards off shore, enemy fire was intense from both medium and minor caliber weapons on the flanks and minor caliber along the beaches. The personnel of these little gunboats displayed magnificent courage as they returned fire with everything they had and refused to move out until they were forced to do so by matériel and personnel casualties. Even then, after undergoing terrific punishment, some

returned to their stations amid a hail of fire, until again heavily hit. Relief LCI(G)'s replaced damaged ships without hesitation. Between 1100 (K) and 1145 (K) all 12 of the LCI(G)'s were hit. LCI *474* ultimately capsized after the crew had been removed, and was ordered sunk. Intensive fire from destroyers and fire support ships, and a smoke screen laid by white phosphorous projectiles, were used to cover this operation. Fire support ships took on board casualties from the LCI(G)'s as they withdrew, and CTG 52.3 in *Terror* most promptly and efficiently intiated emergency repairs for serious hull damage, as well as assisting in care of the wounded. At 1121 (K) *Leutze* was hit, the commanding officer receiving serious injuries, requiring his later transfer to *Estes*, but no extensive damage was sustained by the ship. By 1220 (K) all swimmers of the UDT's but one had been recovered, and the APD's and supporting destroyers moved out of the area. The reconnaissance had been accomplished. It disclosed no underwater or beach obstructions and no mine fields, though one J13 "reef mine" was reported in 8 feet of water off the north flank of Red 2 Beach. Beach and surf conditions were found to be good for landing.

Early in the afternoon heavy fire support ships were ordered to close the western beaches and commence destructive short-range fire. At 1354 (K) three squadrons of land-based bombers of Task Force 93 commenced bombing runs on the objective. The first squadron encountered little large caliber AA fire, but this fire increased in intensity and accuracy as the second and third squadrons commenced their runs. It was learned later that one plane received major damage, and a few others minor damage, but that all were able to return to base. The bombing was conducted from about 5,000 feet altitude, and appeared to be most precise. Under cover of close-in fire support ships with two destroyers in direct support, Sweep Units 5 and 6 swept the area close to the western beaches, without drawing more than sporadic fire from the island. UDT reconnaissance of the western beaches was commenced at 1615 (K). The support was modified in that no LCI(G)'s were used and the destroyers were ordered to close from 3,000 yards to 2,000 yards. A smoke screen by aircraft was ordered but the smoke planes had difficulty in complying, as the screen was not laid until 20 minutes after the order, and was not placed where ordered. The operation was partially screened by white phosphorus projectiles laid on the northern and southern flanks, and behind the beaches. The UDT's accomplished the reconnaissance successfully. One mine was found and a delay charge placed to destroy it. Minefields or underwater obstacles were determined to be nonexistent, and beaches and surf conditions were found to be suitable for landing.

At 1734 (K), *Howard* reported rescuing three men from a crashed TBF. Night deployment commenced about 1830 (K). *Edwards*, *Twiggs*, and *Stembel* were designated to remain at the objective to execute night harassing fire, interdiction of airfields, prevent escape or reinforcement of the garrison, and to maintain careful surveillance of the beaches to ensure that the enemy did no work on them. *Mullany*, APD's of TG 52.4 and Sweep Unit 4 remained with *Estes* in the vicinity of the objective, as did the Gunboat Support Units 1 and 2. Shortly after dark *Twiggs* shot down one enemy plane near the island. At 2321 (K) *Waters* and *Bull* were despatched with beach charts and personnel from the UDT's for distribution and dissemination of information on the beach reconnaissances to CTF 51, CTF 53, and designated elements of the Attack Force. Strikes on Chichi Jima resulted in damage to about 18 small craft and an ammunition barge blown up. At Haha Jima about 15 small and 1 medium-sized craft were damaged. It was estimated, and examination of the afternoon photographs confirmed, that the greater part of major known defensive installations still remained undamaged. However, heavily casemated batteries at the northern base of Suribachi (already on map) and on the right flank of the eastern beaches (3 of the 4 guns not on map) had been definitely located. Orders were issued changing schedules of fire for 18 February to provide for heavy concentration of destructive fire from short range on the blockhouses, pillboxes, etc., of the eastern beach area, and defenses behind it and on each flank. For knocking out the heavy flanking batteries a cross fire by *Idaho* and *Tennessee* was directed. It was felt that unless this was done, the success of the landing itself would be seriously jeopardized, even though it was realized that guns and mortars in other

areas would probably give trouble after the landing. Fire support ships were advised of the entire situation, and directed to make every effort to obtain the greatest possible effect from each remaining round of ammunition and minute of time.

At 0308 (K) on 18 February *Mullany* was sent to rendezvous with *Lunga Point* with photographs for delivery by plane that morning to CTF 51 and various elements of the Attack Force. Minesweeping commenced on schedule. Fire support ships were on station at 0700 (K) and off the eastern beaches delivered almost continuous fire from 0700 (K) to 1830 (K) at ranges of from 1,800 to 3,000 yards from the shore. Other ships fired at targets in other areas throughout the same period. *Texas*, assisted by two destroyers, also covered uncompleted minesweeping operations off the northern shore. During the afternoon a *Texas* spotting plane recovered a downed pilot, uninjured, from 135 miles at sea. He had been sighted by a B29 of the Twenty-first Bomber Command.

Night deployments were commenced at sunset, except that 5 destroyers were assigned to usual night operations at the objective, with special instructions to ensure that no work by the enemy was accomplished on the beaches. By late afternoon all minesweeping necessary to permit a successful landing, and its support and the ensuing unloading, had been accomplished. No mines were found. Reports from firing ships and examination of photographs showed that the principal defensive installations on and behind the eastern beaches, and on their flanks, had been either destroyed or heavily damaged. Among these were included the casemated batteries on the northern and southern flanks of the beaches, which were estimated to have fired on the LCI(G)'s with such telling effect on 17 February. Fragments recovered from LCI(G)'s indicated that the heaviest of these guns were about 150 mm. in caliber. During the evening CTF 52 informed CTF 51 that although weather had prevented expending the full ammunition allowance, and that more installations could be found and destroyed with an additional day of bombardment, he believed a successful landing could be made on 19 February if necessary.

The large staff of an amphibious group commander was needed to achieve coordination of the many and mutually conflicting activities at the objective during the prelanding period. The trained teams which are accustomed to working as a well-knit unit in controlling naval gunfire and support aircraft so that each of these weapons will effectively supplement the other are considered to be a necessity, as are the ample communications, photographic, photo interpretation, map reproduction and housing facilities, and working spaces of an AGC. For this operation the staff was augmented by four assistants in the gunnery section, and one assistant and two photo interpreters in the intelligence section. The services of these additional officers were fully employed and a similar arrangement is strongly recommended for future operations of this type. Familiarity with the problems confronting the Amphibious Force, and the presence of the naval gunfire officer of the staff of the Fifth Amphibious Corps, were of material assistance in modifying plans and methods of attacking defensive installations to suit new developments of the situation as they arose. It is believed that factors discussed above will assume added importance in future prelanding operations of larger scope and greater complexity.

From: Commanding General, Expeditionary Troops (Task Force 56)

Enemy Defensive Tactics

The enemy conducted a position defense which was effective, intense, and notable for its economy of forces. No employment of mobile reserves was encountered. There was no withdrawal through a series of defensive lines; there was, in fact, no significant exposure of enemy troops to our supporting arms. The defense depended on the employment of the maximum number of weapons of all calibers fired continuously from well concealed and protected positions until they were destroyed, reduced, or captured. In the initial stages during the hours of darkness the enemy probed our lines in considerable strength employing smoke to cover his concentrations. This activity declined to limited infiltration attempts as our attack progressed. The decentralized sector defense was complete rather than flexible. However, in spite of the high toll it exacted, the defense failed to realize the full value of its weapons. The enemy's decentralized employment of artillery again demonstrated a failure to coordinate or mass the fires of his many weapons or to transfer fires from registered targets to the many targets of opportunity with accuracy or dispatch. It is worthy of note that the majority of casualties in our assault elements, once the beachhead was established, were caused by the intense and accurate small arms fire—to include knee mortars and grenades.

Limitations of Associated and Supporting Arms

The capture of Iwo Jima would have been impossible without the preparatory bombardment and continued support of fire support vessels, carrier and land-based aircraft supplementing the artillery, rockets, tanks, and organic infantry weapons of the landing force. The record tonnage delivered during the assault was effectively directed in close support, and in coordination with the attack of the infantry.

However, our supporting arms were handicapped in their effectiveness by the geographical limitations of the island, the character of the terrain, and the strength of the enemy defenses. The enemy's heavier installations were frequently impervious to field artillery of light and medium calibers and required the destructive power of high velocity main battery naval gunfire. Artillery was employed both for its destructive effect and to uncover and reveal the location of the many well camouflaged and reinforced caves, bunkers, blockhouses, and pillboxes. The broken configuration of the ground served to mask terrestrial observation, and the natural concealment of enemy positions made air spotting missions difficult. The proximity of our troops to enemy positions, demanded by the exigencies of operations and the necessity to exploit all support, frequently denied us the benefit of adequate heavy fires or bombardment. The coarse volcanic sand in the landing beach areas combined with the nearly impassable topography of Motoyama to impede the movement of tanks, and armored bulldozers had to be used to clear approaches. These tanks, armed with 75-mm. guns and flame throwers, together with self-propelled 75-mm. antitank guns and other antitank weapons, were fired at point-blank ranges.

The result of these limitations was that the burden of reducing many fortifications fell to infantry armed with organic weapons, flame throwers, and demolitions.

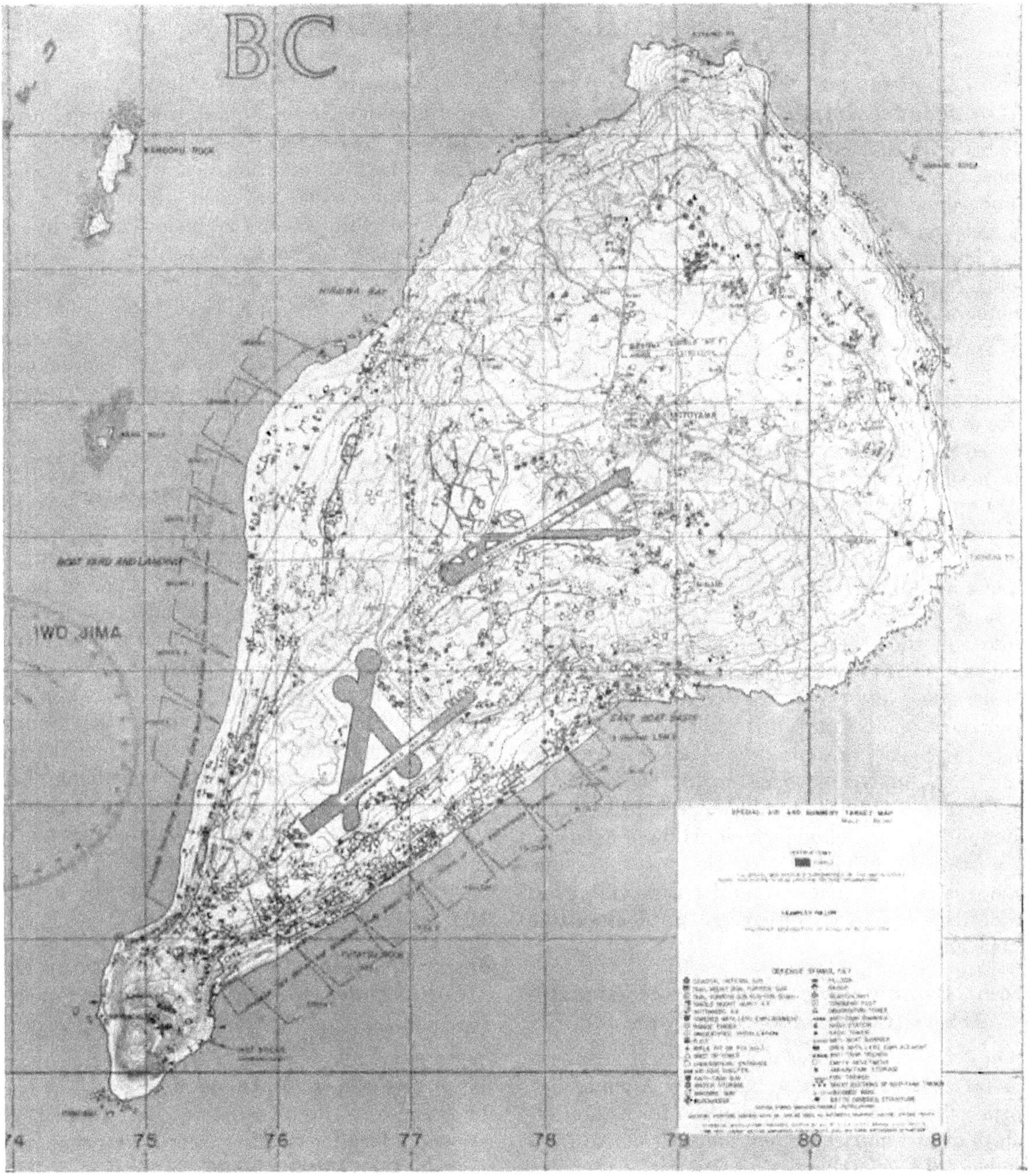
BC
IWO JIMA
74
75
76
77
78
79
80
81

Chapter II. NAVAL GUNFIRE

From: Commander Amphibious Group One (Commander Amphibious Support Force)

This operation clearly demonstrated that previous high altitude bombings and long range bombardment of Iwo Jima directed only into "target areas" achieved negligible damage to the very numerous defenses of the island, which were stout, comparatively small, and well dispersed. Photographic interpretation shows, on the contrary, that the defenses were substantially increased in number during December, January, and early February. The bombardment by this force on 16 and 17 February also had less than the desired effect, due to interference by weather, to the need for giving way to minesweeping and UDT operations, and by lack of thorough familiarity with the actual important targets, as distinguished from a mark on a map, or a photograph. It was not until after fire support ships their spotting planes, and the support aircraft had worked at the objective for 2 days, had become familiar with the location and appearance of the defenses, and had accurately attacked them with close range gunfire and low altitude air strikes, that substantial results were achieved. This experience emphasizes once again the need for ample time as well as ample ships, aircraft, and ammunition, for preliminary reduction of defenses of a strongly defended position. At the same time it is realized that certain defenses will never be destroyed or even discovered until after the troops land.

From: Commanding General, Expeditionary Troops (Commander Task Force 56)

On 8 November, after a more careful study of the target area had been made, V Amphibious Corps submitted a recommendation for a total of 9 days of preliminary bombardment. On 26 November, the Commander, Amphibious Forces, United States Pacific Fleet, replied to this recommendation with a study indicating the necessity of slightly more than 3 days of bombardment, and a statement that the troops would be provided with the best possible preliminary bombardment

consistent with limitations of ammunition supply and time, and the subsequent troop requirements.

On 24 November, V Amphibious Corps requested that 1 additional day of preliminary bombardments be provided. This letter was forwarded with favorable endorsement by the Commanding General, Expeditionary Troops, Fifth Fleet. The Commander, Amphibious Forces, United States Pacific Fleet, forwarded this request, requesting approval provided that there was no objection on the part of the Commander, Fifth Fleet, based on the general strategical situation.

From: Commanding General, Fourth Marine Division, Fleet Marine Force

The Division's concept of NGF requirements for the Iwo Jima operation, which was submitted to VAC LANFOR early in the planning phase, emphasized the necessity for adequate preliminary bombardment of the objective and requested that a minimum of 10 days destructive fire be conducted prior to the landing. It was apparent that in order to insure success of the landing, weapon emplacements, pillboxes, and blockhouses, particularly those located on the right flank of the Division zone of action would have to be reduced prior to D-Day by slow, deliberate, destructive fire from ships firing at close ranges. It is considered that the 3 days allowed for the preliminary bombardment was insufficient.

From: Commander Amphibious Group One (Commander Amphibious Support Force)

Each heavy ship was assigned an area of responsibility, all of which taken together, covered the entire island. Bombardment by destroyers for purposes of destruction was not planned, nor was secondary battery fire from heavy ships contemplated except for counterbattery and UDT cover. The plan provided on D-minus-3 for bombardment at long and medium ranges, not less than 6,000 yards offshore. For this day firing periods were arranged with the view toward having the minimum number of ships firing at one ably a majority of the heavy installations commanding the landing beaches were put out of action prior to H-hour, and little gunfire from fixed guns was experienced.

Three days were allotted to pre-Dog-Day bombardment in order to ensure the destruction of the maximum number of installations and coverage of known positions on the whole island. Sufficient flexibility was allowed in the schedules of fires on these days so that positions stripped of camouflage by heavy caliber fire and discovered by air spot or photographic intelligence could be destroyed, or at least neutralized.

During the pre-Dog-Day bombardment, the intelligence officer of the Amphibious Support Force coordinated all target information. A card was prepared in the following form.

Targets were given a numberical listing (in addition to the location on the air and gunnery target map) and a complete initial list of targets was supplied to each ship in advance of the operation. Additions, deletions and reports were then made by reference to the basic list with a consequent economy of radio transmissions. Targets were assigned to air or naval gunfire as appropriate, and notations and evaluations were based on the report of the ship, plane, air observer or from photo intelligence. On the morning of D-day, the completed target records were delivered to Commander Expeditionary Force, and a transcript to ComLanFor, thereby providing each of them with an up-to-date collection of target information on which to base subsequent deep supporting fires.

ROLLING BARRAGE

Scheduled fires after H-hour were planned to continue for 4 hours and to advance just ahead of the expected line of troop progress. In general, this plan was successful but the troops did not advance as rapidly as the barrage schedule. This required continuous modification of the schedule resulting in repeating fires in certain blocks and delaying the lifting of fires from others.

Shore fire control communications were arranged generally on the same basis as that which worked so successfully in past operations.

As in the past, one frequency was designated "Naval Gunfire Control Net" and used for all gunfire support requests and administrative traffic relative to naval gunfire, except as noted below.

An innovation was the designation of a frequency as the "Naval Gunfire Overload Circuit." This frequency was guarded by the OTC continually so that any ship or shore party concerned with naval gunfire could clear traffic to the OTC when the Gunfire Control Net was crowded. Routine matters such as ammunition reports and reports of firing by ships were handled on the Overload, and this left the main Control Net clear for more important matters.

Another innovation was the "Gunboat Control Net," a separate frequency to handle assignments, reports, and administrative traffic relative to LCI gunboat types, through their task group and unit commanders.

Control of VOF flights was maintained by the Air Spot Control Net (VHF) which was used to handle all administrative matters between the spotting planes and the Naval Gunfire Control Officer. Spotting was done on the regular frequencies and is discussed in greater detail below.

Initial call fire assignments and frequencies were assigned in the Schedule of Fires and were to become effective immediately upon the landing of the Shore Fire Control Parties.

In order to facilitate radio transmissions and prevent error in ammunition reports, a special list of code names was used for all types of ship ammunition including rockets and mortars.

For the close support of the landing, Fire Support Ships were assigned positions between and on the flanks of the landing waves and fire was scheduled as mentioned above. All ships were to maintain at least steerageway except those in the boat lanes while boats were passing. The latter were instructed to clear the boat lanes as soon after How-Hour as it was safe to do so. This fire was to be supplemented by 9 LCI(L)(3)(R)-(RCM)'s, and 18 LCI(M)'s from designated positions, and 12 LCI(G)'s and 12 LCS(L)'s which were to precede the leading wave. Twelve LCI(M)'s were available on call in reserve if needed.

LCI(M) MORTAR PLAN

The rapid rate of fire, high trajectory and long range of the 4".2 chemical mortar were considered to have considerable value for beach preparation fire and for deep support subsequent to How-Hour. Consequently, as recommended following the Marianas operation, an effort was made to develop a craft mounting this weapon and capable of proceeding to the objective under its own power.

Three 4.2 chemical mortars were mounted on an LCI and experiments successfully covered all phases of loading and firing. Additional conversions were made, further tests conducted and standard plans drawn up for delivery of mortar fire.

The schedule of fires for close support prior to How-Hour on Dog-Day provided for mortar fire from designated positions on the flanks of the beaches and after How-Hour deep support, behind the beaches.

AIR SPOT PLAN

VOF planes of VOC–1, a specially trained observation squadron flying CVE-based fighter planes, were available for spotting purposes. These were to be used primarily with destroyers but were available to spot for larger ships if weather prevented use of float planes or if VO of VCS planes were not available.

Because of the high speed at which VOF aircraft travel, it was necessary for the spotter to control the time of firing so that he would be in a position to observe the fall of shot. This did not prove to be a serious handicap and there was no evidence that effectiveness or volume of fire suffered.

VOF planes had a primary and secondary spotting frequency upon which they could transmit and were unable to shift to any HF frequencies other that those two while airborne. A split phone watch was maintained so that a VHF frequency could be guarded simultaneously (Air Spot Control, SAD, FD, etc.).

CALL FIRES

Call fire assignments and communications in general functioned excellently though a bit more complicated than in the past by the addition of VOF spotting planes. The Shore Fire Control Party and air spot supplemented each other on the spotting frequency to achieve better results with the firing ship. In most instances where the plane's transmitter was off frequency, the Shore Fire Control Party and Fire Support Ship tuned their receivers as necessary to receive good signals. In a few cases, ships came up on VHF Air Spot Control Net to facilitate establishing communications on the spotting frequency.

For the first few days, regiments submitted

requests for fire support directly to CTF 52 with resultant confusion and failure to utilize ships to the best advantage. Later it was possible to set up a system whereby divisions submitted requests to the Naval Gunfire Officer attached to Headquarters Landing Force afloat (and later ashore). Based on information previously given him concerning the number and type of ships available, one consolidated request was then submitted to CTF 52. Requests for day assignments were usually submitted prior to 1500 and for night assignments prior to 0400 in order to allow sufficient time to effect any changes or reliefs necessary.

Assignments were addressed by CTF 52 to the ship involved, Landing Force Naval Gunfire Officer, Division Liaison Officer and Regimental Liaison Officer who notified the Battalion Liaison Officer and shore fire control spotter. Frequency to be used, VOF call (if any) and sector from which fire was to be delivered were also designated in the assignment. CTF's 52 and 53 periodically checked the spotting frequencies to see that conditions were satisfactory and, if necessary, assisted in establishing communications.

ILLUMINATION

A large resupply of star shells was provided at the objective since it was anticipated that the demand would be great because of the many caves and irregular terrain which offered excellent opportunities for infiltration during the night. Expectations were fulfilled, for during the period Dog-plus-One through Dog-plus-Eight an average of over 1,000 star shells per night was used.

It is felt that much illumination is still being delivered unnecessarily because of lack of coordination between adjoining battalions in the call for star shells and the desire to maintain constant illumination throughout the night. The best judges of this, however, are division of higher commands ashore.

Notable by its absence was the complaint that empty star shell cases were falling within our own lines. This can be attributed directly to more careful control of line of fire due to greater familiarity on the part of the spotters with star shells and their characteristics.

The LCS(L)(3)'s and LCI(M)'s supported the landing by fire on the beach, behind the beach and on the flanks before and after H-hour. Some were under control of Shore Fire Control Parties after H-hour. The greater part of enemy fire came from the flanks. The 40-mm. fire of the LCI's at caves and cliff areas on the flanks was effective in reducing enemy machine gun fire on the beaches, while rockets and mortar shells helped to keep down short range enemy mortar fire.

LCI(M)'s were very useful for delivering all-night harassing fire. Initially, three divisions were used nightly, gradually tapering off to one or part of one division. These LCI(M)'s usually came under fire from enemy coast guns and intermediate automatic weapon fire intermittently during the night, and it was necessary to detail a cruiser or destroyer to cover each division. None was hit but there were many near misses.

The LCI(L)(3)(R)(RCM)'s were used for harassing and interdiction fires but their rockets were soon exhausted. As there were no replacements available, the LCI(R)'s were used thereafter for RCM and anti-small-craft patrol duties and smoke craft. The rockets have the advantage of long range (4,000–5,250 yards maximum) but their uncertain flight makes the troops unwilling to have them fired over men or boats or very close to front lines.

LCS's were much used to shoot into the ravines which ran down to the coast. This was done at short range and under control of a Shore Fire Control Party or embarked troop officer. Experience shows, however, that the LCS can distinguish the position of our troops and the general situation ashore near the coast better than anyone ashore not in the front lines. Gradually the troops allowed them more and more initiative as their value became apparent. They should, however, always be under control of a Shore Fire Control Party for safety.

From: *Commander Amphibious Group Two* (CTF 53 and CTG 51.21)

4".5 rocket fire for beach preparation and close support of the landing was scheduled for delivery by the Gunboat Support Group consisting of two six-ship LCI(G) units and two six-ship LCS(L) units. The plan provided for initial rocket salvos to be delivered by these ships during the period How-minus-Ninety to How-minus-Forty-five for the purpose of detonating possible beach inflammables well in advance of the time troops would land. The plan also provided

for two full rocket salvos to be delivered in close support of the leading wave. The first of these was to be delivered on the beach at How-minus-Ten-minutes after which launchers were to be reloaded and the second salvo fired 300 to 500 yards inland from the beach. Strafing by aircraft, scheduled to commence at How-minus-five-minutes, required the second 4".5 rocket salvo to be fired prior to this time.

To prevent early blanketing of supporting fire of two destroyers and a battleship stationed in the boat lanes, the plan prescribed that the four six-ship gunboat units proceed toward shore in unit columns ahead of the leading LVT assault wave. After passing the battleship-destroyer line, the gunboat units were to deploy into line for firing rockets.

Of the original 12 LCI(G)'s of Gunboat Support Units No. 1 and No. 2, only 3 were in condition to deliver the scheduled support on Dog-Day, the others having been lost or damaged by enemy fire on previous days. Units No. 3 and No. 4 consisting of 6 LCS(L)'s each were directed to increase their spacing on final deployment in order to cover the portions of the beach assigned by plan to the absent LCI(G)'s.

On completion of their rocket salvos at How-minus-Five-minutes, four LCS(L)'s of each of the two gunboat support units took position according to plan, opposite the flanks of the landing area and supported, with 40-mm. fire, battalions to which initially assigned. This fire was directed on the slopes of Suribachi Yama and the high flanking ground on the right of the beach. Until communications were established with assigned spotters ashore, fire was directed by replacement spotters previously embarked in one LCS(L) of each unit for this purpose.

Mortar Support Units No. 1, No. 2, and No. 5, consisting of six mortar LCI's, were assigned to provide scheduled flanking and deep supporting mortar fire as follows: Units No. 2 and No. 5, using plan "A," fired from How-minus-Thirty-five to How-minus-Seven-minutes on the eastern slopes and approaches to Suribachi Yama while Unit No. 1, using the same fire delivery plan, delivered fire on the eastern flank high ground during the same period. At How-Hour Units No. 2 and No. 5 in column, entered and crossed the boat lanes from the west, turned shoreward into line and followed the Sixth assault wave toward shore.

At about How-plus-Twenty-minutes, when 2,000 yards from shore all ships of these two units opened fire using plan B with mortar range set for 3,200 yards and swept a rectangular area 2,200 yards long by 1,000 yards deep as they moved in. Stopping and lying to 1,000 yards from shore, fire was then maintained 1,800 yards inland and parallel to the beach until How-plus-Sixty-minutes. At How-minus-Seven, Mortar Support Unit No. 1 shifted its line of fire farther to the east for safety to troops and resumed fire at How-plus-Ten-minutes firing at a reduced rate for neutralization until 1,300; 17,400 rounds of 4″2 mortar were scheduled for delivery in support of the landing by these three units.

RCM and Rocket Support Unit No. 1 consisting of nine 5″0 SSR Rocket LCI's, delivered scheduled neutralization fire on the Motoyama area from 0645 to 1300. All rockets on board these ships (a total of approximately 9,500) were delivered during this period, using standard plan RA from a reference point to northeast of the island. On completion of this fire, all fire support duties of this unit terminated for the remainder of the operation.

The eight LCS(L)'s assigned to flank battalions continued their close fire support missions throughout the day, replacement 40-mm. ammunition being obtained for them from heavy cruisers. For night support, four LCS(L)'s of Unit No. 3 were assigned to support battalions designated by Division Headquarters.

On completion of their scheduled fire, Mortar Support Units No. 1, No. 2, and No. 5 replenished mortar ammunition and joined Units No. 3 and No. 4 in area Roger awaiting assignment. Night harassing mortar fire requests from Headquarters Landing Force were fulfilled by assignment of Units No. 2 and No. 5 to cover prescribed areas throughout the night using standard plan A and varying the line of fire between specified limits. A total of 24,000 rounds of which 20 percent was WP, were delivered by these two units from reference points 1,000 yards off the northwest and southeast coasts of the island. Large caliber enemy counter fire was received by the northern unit, but was not intense or accurate enough to require the withdrawal of this unit.

LCS(L)'s of Unit No. 4 and LCI(G)'s available from RCM Unit No. 2 were assigned daily to support battalions designated by Headquarters

Landing Force. Division intelligence officers, specially trained observers, and naval gunfire liaison officers were frequently embarked in ships for reconnaissance and specific fire missions along the shore lines in advance of troop movement. On March 8 all LCS(L)'s departed the area. On March 12, in anticipation of possible attempt by the enemy to effect evacuation of high ranking Japanese by submarine, an LCI(G) was ordered to patrol the coast line beyond our lines to observe for and prevent any such attempt. This patrol was continued nightly thereafter until the island was secure.

One Mortar Unit continued to be assigned each night to deliver harassing fire. Enemy counter fire continued to require the assignment of a destroyer or cruiser to provide support for the harassing unit. On departure of Units No. 1, No. 2, and No. 5 from the area on February 26, Units No. 3 and No. 4 were reorganized into five-ship divisions. Due to the reduced size of the remaining units and their inexperience in plan A fire delivery, night harassing fires were hereafter delivered using plan C. On 28 February, two more mortar LCI's departed the area, leaving two four-ship units available for mortar fire. On 27 February and for several days thereafter individual mortar LCI's were assigned during daylight to provide direct support to battalions designated by Headquarters Landing Force.

The remaining area into which night harassing fire could safely be delivered, required the employment of only one mortar LCI on the night of 1 March. Thereafter harassing fires at night by these ships was discontinued. On 3 March all remaining mortar LCI's departed the area.

Ammunition expenditures by LCI types exclusive of pre-Dog-Day expenditures, were as follows:

4″2 mortar	60, 000
4″5 BR rockets	8, 000
40-mm	116, 000
5″0 SSR rockets	9, 500

GUNBOATS (LCI(G)'s AND LCS(L)(3)'s)

Heretofore in Central Pacific operations the ship-to-shore movement support by LCI gunboats has consisted of one full rocket salvo delivered on the beach at about How-minus-Ten minutes. At Iwo Jima the gunboat group made an early run toward shore between How-minus-Ninety and

How-minus-Forty-five and delivered initial rocket salvos in an attempt to detonate possible inflammables on the beach well in advance of the time of landing. Another innovation at Iwo Jima was the loading and firing of a second rocket salvo during the ship-to-shore movement of the leading wave. The gunboats fired their first salvo at How-minus-Ten minutes as in past operations, then reloaded rocket racks as they moved in to a range of 600–700 yards from the beach and fired a second salvo at How-minus-Five minutes placing this salvo 300 to 500 yards inland. Since 4″.5 rocket fire is more neutralizing than destructive and since its short range prevents its use for neutralization of inland areas, its use has rarely been requested after a landing. The best employment of 4″.5 rockets therefore is beach neutralization just prior to the landing and their employment for initial and additional salvos at Iwo Jima is recommended for future landing support.

Prearranged fire schedules provided for the initial assignment of one gunboat unit to support each of the two flank battalions on the beach. Replacement naval gunfire liaison officers and spotters were embarked in the gunboat unit flagship to direct the fire until communications were established with the spotter ashore. This plan provided an excellent neutralizing fire on the flanks of the landing beach and was found to be so effective that the Landing Force requested continuous assignment of one or more gunboats to the battalion on the flanks of the front line for the remainder of the operation.

MORTAR LCI's

This was the first operaton in which LCI's mounting mortars have been employed by the Fifth Amphibious Force. Their primary mission, as conceived in the initial planning, was the delivery of heavy harassing fire at night to prevent the initiation of organized counterattacks. Their support with this fire was most gratifying and materially reduced the demands for harassing fire by destroyers and cruisers.

Two methods of delivering harassing mortar fire at night were employed at Iwo Jima: (1) Plan A of the standard mortar fire plans, in which five LCI's steam on an eliptical track around an LCI acting as reference ship. Ships fire singly in succession during the two minutes' run on the leg

on which they are pointed toward the target area. (2) Plan C in which the six LCI's of a division lie to on a line, 200 yards between ships, and fire when the ship's head is between prescribed limiting lines of fire. Both plans have many advantages and disadvantages. Since it is next to impossible to hold an LCI on an accurate heading for a long period when dead in the water, plan C is unsuitable for interdiction fire where continuous and fairly accurate fire along a definite line is required. Harassing fire, which requires irregular volume and rate of fire with an unsystematic pattern and coverage of the area harassed, is especially typical of the fire to be expected of six LCI's dead in the water all on different headings between prescribed limits. (Plan A, on the other hand, has all the fire delivery characteristics most suited for interdiction fire and least suited for harassing fire.

The 3,200-yard range limit of LCI mortar fire requires these ships to approach as close to shore as safe navigation permits in order to place their fire as far inland as possible. On a well defended island such as Iwo Jima, this close approach to shore drew considerable enemy fire even at night. LCI mortar ships found good use for their bow 40-mm. in delivery of counterbattery fire in self-protection, but this was found insufficient and it became necessary to assign one of the general support destroyers or cruisers to cover the nightly harassing mortar LCI unit. In making plans for delivery of night (or day) harassing fire by mortar LCI's, the plans should incorporate the employment of a destroyer, for counter-battery protection of the harassing unit. This ship should work with the Mortar Unit Commander on a common frequency.

On request, individual mortar LCI's were assigned to battalions for direct support, generally to those battalions whose flanks were along the shoreline as in the case of gunboat support. Preliminary reports indicate that this support was more in the form of harassing or neutralization fire for the battalion supported. In rough water, the accuracy of LCI mortar fire in deflection is greatly decreased by rolling and cannot be safely called for in areas close to own troops. LCI mortar fire for direct support should therefore only be expected to accomplish harassing or preparation neutralizing fire for an advance into areas within range of the LCI mounted mortar.

COMINCH P-0012

While the accuracy in deflection of mortar fire from LCI's is greatly affected by rolling and variations in ship head, its accuracy in range is quite dependable and relatively unaffected by motion of the ship. It is therefore very suitable for neutralizing fire over the heads of troops when the line of fire is perpendicular to the line of troops. Its high trajectory makes it ideal for use when ships and troops located between the target and firing ships preclude the use of high velocity flat trajectory fire. At Iwo Jima, the neutralization of large areas inland from the beaches was effectively delivered by mortar fire from LCI's on a line parallel to and 1,000 yards from shore. This fire was not provided however, until How-plus-Twenty minutes. Using Plan B with desired modifications, mortar LCI's should be employed in the boat lanes to provide beach neutralization just prior to the time the first wave leaves the line of departure and during its run to the beach. They should precede the first wave by any desired distance, stop and lie to not less than 600 yards (minimum firing range) from shore, and continue mortar fire on the beach until the first wave is about 200 yards from shore. At this time the fire should be lifted about 200 to 500 yards inland and lifted in predetermined steps thereafter according to a prearranged time schedule based on anticipated troop advance. This type of moving close support was provided at Iwo Jima using 5"/38 AA Common fire with 1,200-foot second charges.

From: Commander Cruiser Division Thirteen

The enemy knew from the terrain that the landings would have to come on the southeastern or southwestern beaches. He planned his defenses to resist to the utmost the advance up the long axis of the island.

(a) He built defenses with an eye to naval gunfire, particularly to close fire. The terrain lent itself admirably. Few positions were built which could be reached by close-in fire because the trajectories were too flat at short ranges.

(b) He also built against bombing by constructing a surprising number of small strongpoints, interconnecting but individual, so that bomb damage would be confined to a small area. That is, he dispersed but multiplied defense positions.

(c) He played a very intelligent game in the use of weapons prior to and after the landing. He made all his guns count, seldom fired unless he had a good target; kept his flak positions concealed. He hid his mortars, antitank and inactive guns, until they could be used to advantage.

(d) Thus he concealed his strength so that on D-day the United States High Command was in a good deal of doubt as to what the opposition would be despite the long period of softening up and the vast amount of effort expended in advance.

From: Commander Task Force Fifty-four—Commander Amphibious Group Eleven

It was obvious from the outset that the enemy defensive situation was one of the strongest yet encountered in this theater; that blockhouses, pillboxes, and caves were constructed and situated not only to meet a land attack but to withstand heavy naval gunfire. Moreover, the enemy must be credited with unusual and painstaking concealment of vital defenses and gun positions. Our intelligence photos were good but they could not be expected to show what neither the eye nor the camera lens could see.

Against such defenses, long or medium-range gunfire simply is not effective, and a tremendous amount of valuable ammunition can be wasted in general area fire. The reasons are twofold: First, the above mentioned concealment and camouflage make the location of targets possible only at very close range; above-target plane observation is not very effective for this purpose. Secondly, even when discovered, targets are so reinforced by a mass of earthworks that extremely heavy close range fire is required to uncover them before the essential job of destruction is begun; area fire seems to have had a very limited effect in this regard. Though a certain amount of general area fire is necessary initially to shake up the enemy and permit approach to closer ranges, doctrinal trust in neutralization fire may have to be revised.

The hard unpleasant fact must be acknowledged that direct hits must be scored repeatedly. This necessitates close point-blank ranges and acute observation. Naturally, this involves the threat of coast defense guns, but the risk of enemy hits may have to be accepted to do the job. At Iwo Jima enemy fire on our heavy ships was unexpectedly light even though firing positions less than 2,000 yards off shore were frequent after Dog-minus-3-Day. Observation of the medium range bombardment executed on Dog-minus-3 showed little apparent damage.

From: Commanding Officer U. S. S. "Tuscaloosa" (CA)

It is believed that more attention and time should be devoted to *training* gun pointers and trainers in elementary pointer fire. Pointer fire appeared to be far below the peacetime standard of the old short range battle practices. The present emphasis in training is almost entirely on the various methods of director control which, of course, are the primary methods of shooting. However, well-pointed local control fire can be effective at close ranges, and occasion will arise when director control is not available.

From: Commanding Officer U. S. S. "New York" (BB 34)

The construction and positioning of defensive installations such as pill boxes, blockhouses, coastal batteries, and antiaircraft installations necessitated in every case a direct hit or many near hits to complete their destruction. Spotting on the 16th and 17th was by ship's planes and on the 18th range was closed to 1,750 yards, and spotting was by both plane and ship. The last day of bombardment was most effective because of the great facility with which targets could be identified and salvos could be spotted, and also because of the large quantity of ammunition expended on targets by the 14″/45 caliber and 5″/51 caliber batteries.

From: Commanding Officer U. S. S. "Nevada" (BB)

The enemy installations on Iwo Jima were very well camouflaged and of very heavy construction. The larger ones could be destroyed or severely damaged only by repeated hits with the main battery. At ranges from 1,500 to 2,500 yards these targets could be distinguished by ship's spotters and gun pointers and trainers. Pointer fire was most effective as the fall of shot and results could be clearly seen. Most of the damage done to enemy installations by *Nevada*'s gun fire was accomplished at short ranges with pointer fire.

The 40-mm. battery was used against a variety of targets including caves, suspected machine gun emplacements, light artillery emplacements and on one occasion against a small number of enemy personnel. The 40-mm. fire was believed to be effective only as a harassing agent. On the one occasion against enemy personnel, about six men were observed abandoning a damaged block house and were strafed with 40-mm. fire.

From: Commanding Officer U. S. S. "Pringle" (DD 477)

Fire support area was overcrowded and in the later phases wedged tight inshore between the transports. With a cross wind and current the problem of holding the proper heading was very difficult. The firing bearings at low elevations for the DD445 class are quite limited. To avoid having to swing ship with a loaded gun, it is necessary to consult some elaborate firing cam data before giving the order to load. No answer can be given to the problem, but to have the figures on hand, watch how the ship is swinging and load accordingly. The decrease in the rate of fire is unavoidable.

From: Commanding Officer U. S. S. "Van Valkenburgh" (DD 656)

During the bombardment, this vessel closed within 600 yards of the beach in order to pick up targets visually, but with little or no success. Targets were evidently well obscured and observation by the shore fire control party was very difficult, most of the time impossible. White phosphorus was used almost continuously, while it lasted, to aid the spotters. This vessel received no fire from shore installations, but observed some mortar and machinegun fire from the beach in other fire support sectors.

From: Commanding Officer U. S. S. "Bennett" (DD 473)

The commanding officer was distressed by the failure of certain "Oboes" and "Charlies" to realize the critical ammunition situation. On 22 February, between 0835 and 0910, this vessel, in accordance with instructions of the "Oboe", fired rapid four-gun salvos for preparation fire. The fire was unobserved. Three times the "Oboe" was informed of the continuing fire, and three times orders were received to keep it up. When fire was checked at 0910, a total of 587 rounds of AA common had been expended. It is realized that a high rate of fire is necessary in preparation fire, but it is believed this expenditure was excessive for an unobserved area of doubtful targets.

On 27 February an "Oboe" ordered this vessel to fire one two-gun salvo per minute (harassing fire) until further notice and then checked out of the net. He was off the net from 1235 to 1356. The commanding officer questions the wisdom of such a practice, not only because of excessive expenditure of ammunition, but also because of the danger of unobserved, uncontrolled fire near our own lines.

From: Commander Mortar Support Group 52.6 (Commander LCI Flotilla Twenty-one)

Plan ABLE consists of sustained fire covering a comparatively narrow target area and capable of extension in range. This plan is best adapted for close supporting fire (flank protection), harassing and interdiction fire. This plan of fire is delivered from a predetermined reference point around which the ships circle, delivering fire when the firing ship is headed toward the target area. The ships circle in both clockwise and counterclockwise movements, depending on the tactical situation.

Plan BAKER consists of a barrage fire covering a wide target area and capable of progressive movement in range. It is best adapted for neutralization fire and close support fire over and beyond our own troops. This plan of fire is delivered from a predetermined point with the ships that are firing disposed on a line of bearing parallel to the desired range median of the barrage or in line abreast formation.

Plan CHARLIE consists of independent or minor concentration fire covering point targets or targets of opportunity. It is best adapted for harassing fire, counter-battery fire, interdiction fire, and incidental destruction fire, particularly that requiring high trajectory. It is conducted by single or several ships whose fire may or may not be coordinated depending on assignment and is delivered from a reference point and bearing from the designated target area.

All target areas and fire plans in connection with the mission were contained in the Operations Plan, up to and including H-hour-plus-60. Subsequently, target fire and smoke missions were assigned.

At the outset of the mission it was assumed that preliminary naval and air bombardment had effectively silenced coastal defense and shore batteries that could possibly interfere with the carrying out of this group's mission. This assumption was subsequently found to be true. Sporadic mortar and machine gun fire was encountered however, which interfered with our operations on several occasions.

From: Commander Amphibious Forces, United States Pacific Fleet (Commander Joint Expeditionary Force)

GENERAL EFFECT OF NAVAL GUNFIRE BOMBARDMENT

Practically all enemy fixed installations capable of firing upon the landing beaches or transport areas and boat lanes were well covered and either destroyed or neutralized prior to How-Hour as evidenced by lack of opposition to the landing of first waves on all but Red Beaches. Many of the installations in caves or strongly reinforced positions were destroyed regardless of ammunition expenditure. A few fixed installations were later put back into commission and caused trouble for short periods.

The following lessons are either new or received additional emphasis at Iwo:

(*a*) Enemy mortars are very difficult to locate and destroy.

(*b*) Indirect naval gunfire is inaccurate when firing to hit on hill tops with indirect fire. This is because of long range and unknown inequalities of terrain.

(*c*) Guns emplaced in caves are difficult to destroy even when location is known.

(*d*) Observation of SFCP's is inaccurate in rolling and irregular terrain, and when greatly displaced laterally from the gun-target line. The SFCP's should therefore be located on the highest points, and as close as possible with respect to the gun-target line.

(*e*) Enemy powder produces little or no smoke and flame. SFCP's planes and ships therefore have difficulty in locating enemy guns. On the other hand, our powder causes much smoke and flame, both afloat and ashore.

(*f*) For destroying heavy emplacements and other vertical targets, very short range deliberate fire is required. This does not mean that long range plunging fire is not advantageous under certain other condition.

Ammunition Resupply and Expenditure Data

The following table gives the amounts of ammunition replaced and expended at Iwo Jima:

Resupply	16″ HC	14″ HC	12″ HC	8″ HC	6″ HC	5″ AAC	5″ Star	5″ Rkt	4.5 BR	4.2 Mor
From assault ships				5,400		27,500	1,500			32,000
From AE's and AKE's		400		1,300	2,750	46,000	4,800			
Total resupply		400		6,700	2,750	73,500	6,300			32,000

Expended	16″ HC	14″ HC	12″ HC	8″ HC	6″ HC	5″ AAC	5″ Star	5″ Rkt	4.5 BR	4.2 Mor
D-minus-3 to D-day		3,300	1,000	3,500	1,900	14,000	200			
D-day	1,950	1,500	400	1,700	2,000	31,000	1,500	12,000	8,000	20,000
D-plus-1 through D-plus-17*	450	900		6,200	4,500	102,000	13,000		2,000	50,000
D-plus-18 to D-plus-35				300		5,000	3,000			
Total expended	2,400	5,700	1,400	11,700	8,400	152,000	17,700	12,000	10,000	70,000
Tons	2,280	3,640	520	2,020	440	4,160		270	145	875

Total tons 14,250.

Statistics

	16″ HC	14″ HC	12″ HC	8″ HC	6″ HC	5″ AAC	5″ Star	5″ Rkt	4.5 BR	4.2 Mor
Average daily rounds of call and harassing fires D-plus-1 through D-plus-17	26	53	0	341	265	6,000	765	0	118	4,550

*LCI(M)'s departed D-plus-12.

It is interesting to note that a total of 14,250 tons were fired at Iwo Jima as compared with 10,965 tons at Saipan.

659889—45——5

**HEAVILY PROTECTED DEFENSES DESTROYED BY DELIBERATE
CLOSE RANGE NAVAL GUNFIRE**

Reinforced Concrete Pill Box

Pillbox With Machine Gun.

Covered Artillery Position.

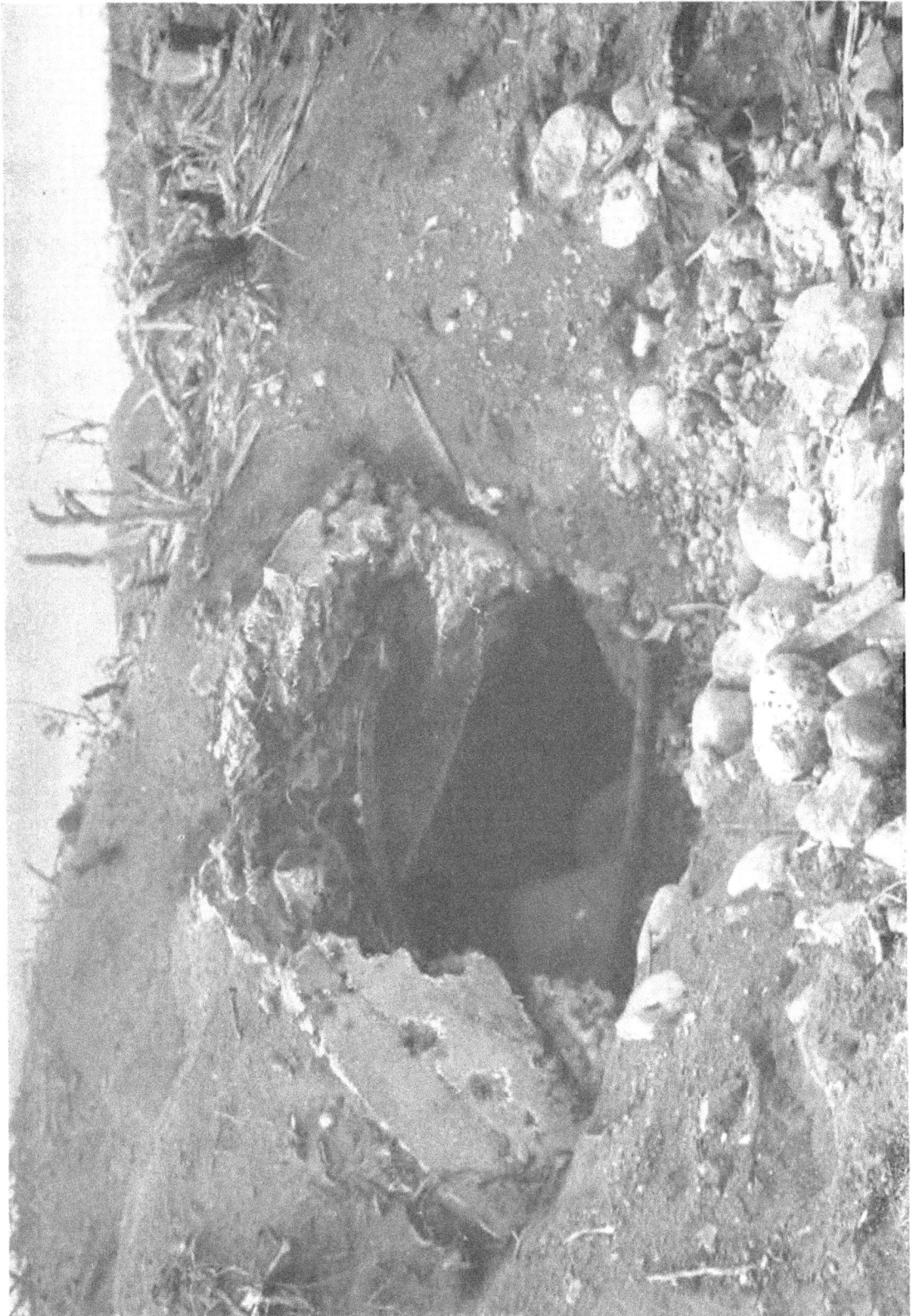

Reinforced Concrete Gun Position.

Covered Artillery Position. Note Concrete and Planted Grass.

Battery at Base of Suribachi.

Battery at Base of Suribachi.

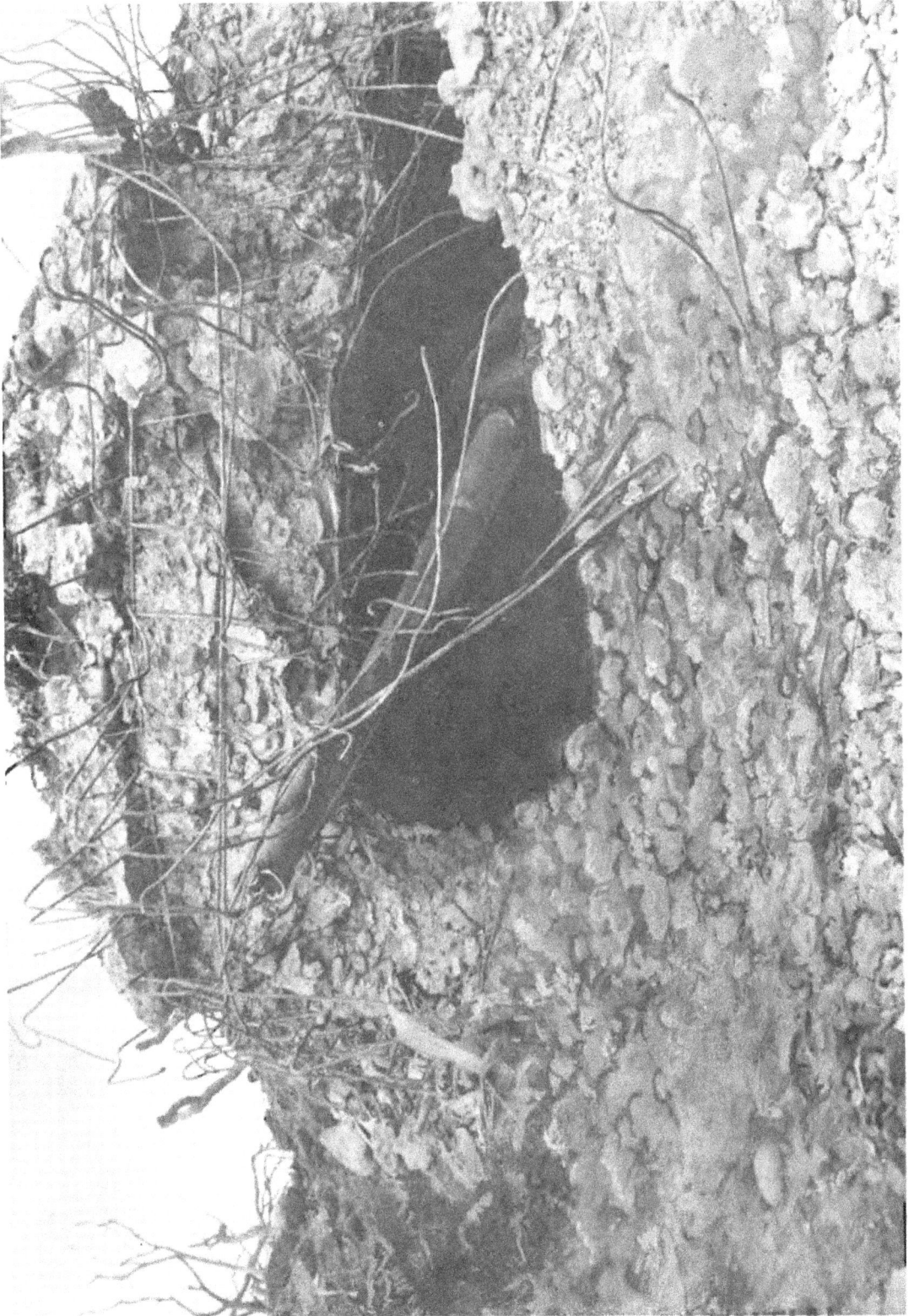

Coastal Defense Gun.

Reinforced Concrete CD Emplacement, TA 183X D-Plus-14.

Chapter III. AIR SUPPORT

*From: Commander Amphibious Forces,
United States Pacific Fleet (Commander
Joint Expeditionary Force)*

PRELIMINARY AIR BOMBARDMENT

Preliminary air bombardment of Iwo Jima was delivered by heavy horizontal bombers operating from the Marianas bases. A long series of area bombing missions were flown during the months preceding the landing.   From Dog-minus-Twenty this bombardment was conducted on the basis of target requests issued by Commander Joint Expeditionary Force. The principles involved in specifying the targets for preliminary air bombardment were:

(*a*) The neutralization of the airfields and installations on Iwo Jima.

(*b*) The destruction of gun positions and fixed defenses.

(*c*) Unmasking of additional targets.

Although the tonnage of bombs was large, no permanent results apparently were obtained. The southern portion of Iwo Jima is soft volcanic sand which easily craters but is just as easily smoothed out again. On the north it is rocky and has many steep ravines. The Japs were well dug in and only those bombs which hit the few exposed targets, or hit and penetrated protected ones, did any lasting damage. So far as can be determined the psychological gain from the prolonged bombardment could not be measured in terms of reduced efficiency on the part of the Japs on the day of the landing.

*From: Commanding General, Headquarters
Fourth Marine Division, Fleet Marine
Force*

Results indicate that high horizontal bombing by land based aircraft had little effect on the enemy's defensive system. In fact, one POW estimated that 40 percent of the bombs dropped by these aircraft prior to D-day missed the island entirely and this is considered a conservative figure.   In order to permit more effective air strikes from low altitudes, which are essential if destruction of emplacements is to be accomplished, early destruction of enemy AA defenses must be effected. The efficiency of NGF spotting by VOS aircraft would also be enhanced by the reduction of the enemy's AA.

*From: Commanding General, Expeditionary
Troops (Task Force 56)*

The prolonged aerial bombardment of Iwo Jima, which was a daily occurrence for over 70 days, had no appreciable effect in the reduction of the enemy's well prepared and heavily fortified defensive installations.

*From: Commander Fire Support Unit Four
(54.1.4) (Commander Cruiser Division Five)*

On D-minus-2-Day, three flights of B–24's bombed Iwo from about 5,000 feet, the surface ships suspending fire during the runs of the B–24's. The first group received meager AA fire; but the second and third received moderate to heavy at times; though none of the planes were noticed to be in difficulty. On D-day, one group of B–24's (15 in number) bombed at about 4,000 feet while the ships continued their bombardment. By observation, no AA fire was delivered at the B–24's. This one group was the only attack in the 60 days of bombing delivered at low altitude. The surface ships could have coordinated their bombardments with the air bombings throughout this 60-day period; and it is estimated that many more surface bombardments could have been undertaken with the same surface composition. By this means, the major effort, which was in the B–24's, could have been greatly increased in accuracy and effectiveness.

*From: Commander Amphibious Forces,
United States Pacific Fleet (Commander
Joint Expeditionary Force)*

Relative effectiveness of the weapons at the disposal of air were:

(*a*) **Machine gun .50-caliber bullets.**—These were the principal weapons of fighters of the ex-CAP and fighter spotters. Strafing was effective against exposed enemy troops and gunners but not against the many who were well dug in.

(b) **GP bombs.**—These were the standard weapons of air bombardment. All of the enemy's above-ground installations were destroyed but his strong points resisted bombing.

(c) **Napalm.**—This new weapon has given excellent results in previous operations but at Iwo a large percentage of duds were observed. The cause of the duds is not known. The Napalm which ignited was apparently effective.

(d) **Rockets.**—The ability of rockets to hit and penetrate fortified positions was thoroughly demonstrated in this operation. Rockets were in constant demand and their use made them the most successful air weapons in the Iwo Jima campaign.

From: Commander Fire Support Unit Four (54.1.4) (Commander Cruiser Division Five)

In the period about 60 days prior to D-minus-3-Day, the B–24 force in the Marianas (search planes, night snoopers, and surface craft) operated against Iwo and its communications.

While there was unity of command in the higher echelon, by the time it reached the operational forces it was command by cooperation (though willing and good as far as it went). The surface forces conducted six heavy bombardments against Iwo, and one against Chichi Jima and Haha Jima. Ten medium tonnage ships of various types (DE, APD, LST, LSM, small AK, one trawler) were sunk or destroyed. The B–24's bombed for about 60 consecutive days, releasing at 18,000- to 20,000-foot altitude usually against AA. fire. Once or twice a group of B–29's assisted. The night attack planes against shipping seldom located targets. The day search planes frequently reported convoys headed toward or away from Chichi Jima.

From: Commander Amphibious Forces, United States Pacific Fleet (Commander Joint Expeditionary Force)

The planes used in supporting the Iwo Jima operation were furnished by CVE and Fast Carrier Units. An innovation in this operation was the use of a specially trained Antisubmarine

Patrol Squadron for day and night patrols. A CVE was devoted to this phase of air support. One night operations carrier was provided from Task Force 58 to supply dusk and night target combat air patrol. This carrier also provided a dusk and dawn sweep to neutralize Susaki airfield, Chichi, Haha and Minami Jima. The escort carriers (TG 52.2) were divided into four units as follows:

TU 52.2.1—6 CVE's.
TU 52.2.2—4 CVE's.
TU 52.2.3—2 CVE's.
TU 52.2.5—1 CV (reported from TF 58 on D-plus-Two).

The number of CVE's at the target area was as follows:

9 CVE's from D-minus-Three through D-minus-One.
11 CVE's from D-Day through D-plus-Two.
10 CVE's from D-plus-Three through D-plus-Eight.
11 CVE's from D plus Nine.

Direct air support operations Iwo Jima began on D-minus-Three with the arrival of TG 52 and 54. The Advance Commander Air Support Control Units was embarked in the *Estes*. This was the first operation in which the Advance Commander Air Support Control Unit worked from an AGC and with a complete team. The results were more satisfactory than in previous amphibious operations where it was necessary to operate from battleships or other naval vessels.

The pre-Dog-Day air support consisted of Combat Air Patrol, Anti-Submarine Patrol, direct support to Minesweepers and Underwater Demolition Teams, Smoking and Photographic missions, and heavy bombing strikes by land based Army aircraft. In addition, regular air support groups were available on schedule throughout the day for covering missions and called strikes.

TIME OF COMPLETING ASSIGNED MISSIONS

In almost all cases, an accurate record was taken of the time a mission was assigned, and the time it was completed. Following is a break-down of the times taken to complete assigned missions:

From: *Commander Amphibious Forces, United States Pacific Fleet (Commander Joint Expeditionary Force)*

Time of assignment to time of completion:	Number of missions
Under 15 minutes	66
15 to 30 minutes	67
31 to 45 minutes	33
46 to 60 minutes	8
Over 60 minutes	8
Unknown	6
	188

DIRECT AIR SUPPORT OF GROUND FORCES—CONTROLLED BY LFASCU

Commander Landing Force Air Support Control Unit assumed control of direct support aircraft at the objective on 1 March 1945 at 1000. Support aircraft assigned to shore-based control consisted of air coordinators, tactical air observers, strike groups, relieved combat air patrols and VOF flights, and miscellaneous photographic, spray and other utility missions. Effective with commencement of operations from Maple Field 8 March, control was also exercised over land-based transport, evacuation, supply-drop and transient aircraft.

OY OBSERVATION PLANES

A total of 18 OY type observation planes were brought to Iwo Jima for VMO Squadrons 4 and 5. It was not possible to load planes for the Third Division at Saipan as originally intended. Six of these spotting planes were carried on the LST 776 which was equipped with Brodie launching and recovery gear. The second plane launched from the LST crashed into the sea because of a temporary failure of the launching gear. The remaining 12 planes were carried by 6 of the CVE's. (Two were lost in the sinking of the *Bismarck Sea*.)

From: *Commander Amphibious Forces, United States Pacific Fleet (Commander Joint Expeditionary Force)*

COORDINATION WITH NAVAL GUNFIRE AND ARTILLERY

In spite of early misgivings, coordination between air support, naval gunfire, and artillery did not prove to be a major problem. Due to the small size of the objective and the close ranges fired by ships and artillery, it was very

seldom necessary to use plan "VICTOR" or plan "NEGAT."

NAVAL GUNFIRE

During the early hours of D-day, a graphic plot of preplanned high-ordinate naval gunfire was available to SAD control officers. This enabled them to direct strikes into areas that gunfire was not covering, or to hold planes to a safe minimum altitude. After the pre planned gunfire phase was completed, close liaison in the joint operations room was adequate for obtaining information on all missions that might have been endangered by high-ordinate gunfire. After control of high-ordinate rocket and mortar landing craft fire was passed from CTF 51 to CTF 53 (about D-plus-One), liaison on gunfire matters was not satisfactory. However, high-ordinate gunfire was used so seldom at this time that pilots experienced little difficulty in performing missions.

ARTILLERY

Accurate coordination with artillery was practically impossible because there was no Corps Artillery representative on the *Eldorado*. It was only the fact that there was so little high-ordinate artillery fire that enabled SAD officers to send planes on missions without a detailed check on artillery. Artillery communication in the joint operations room proved too slow and cumbersome in the few cases where plan "NEGAT" was requested. In one instance (mission No. 8 on D-plus-Two), it took 30 minutes to get a reply over artillery circuits to a request for a plan "NEGAT." The reply, when received, stated that another 25 minutes would be required to place "NEGAT" in effect. Since planes on station could not wait that long, they were directed on the mission. (In this case the SAD officer estimated that the artillery ordinate in the target area would not be too high to be dangerous). In a later request for plan "NEGAT" (mission No. 7 on D-plus-Three), much better results were made by contacting the Landing Force over ASC net. In this case, it took only 20 minutes to clear with Corps Artillery for a low-level Napalm and strafing attack.

The Iwo Jima operation marked the first time that the Brodie Sea Rig for launching and recovering small artillery spotting aircraft has been available for use in combat. This system, constructed on an LST, enables the LST to carry, launch and recover 6 to 10 small planes in addition to carrying a tank deck load of cargo. Prior to launching, the plane is suspended from a trolley mounted between 2 booms suspended clear of the ship's side 40 feet over the water. In launching, the plane runs the length of the trolley and trips a hook release; in recovery, the plane flies parallel to the ship, hooking onto a trapeze loop, and is braked to a stop along the trolley. At Iwo Jima 5 of the 6 planes carried were launched successfully, but due to rough weather no recoveries were attempted by the LST and the planes were landed on the island.

From: Commander Amphibious Group Two (CTF 53 and CTG 51.21)

For the first time in an amphibious operation in this theater an Air Support Control Unit was landed and set up ashore with the intention of actively controlling close troop support missions. This unit was composed of marine and naval officers (with the former predominating) and marine enlisted technicians and operators. The liaison that this unit was able to accomplish by virtue of the proximity (75 feet) to the Landing Force Command Post far surpassed anything that has ever gone before in air support operations and as a result, troop requests for air support were run much more expeditiously than ever before. It is considered that a Landing Force Air Support Control Unit is an absolute necessity for the control of troop support missions. However, it is felt that the Landing Force Air Support Control Unit tried to assume the control of close support missions before they had monitored all the nets long enough to get the routine and to pick up control without any lost motion. Some equipment difficulties entered into the picture since this was the first service use of the radios. It is felt that in future operations when the LFASCU is preparing to assume control of troop support missions, they should monitor all nets which they expect to operate for a minimum of 12 hours. At quiet periods, radio checks should be made. Net control officers expecting to join the LFASCU for the operation of the major strike nets (SAD–1, SAD–2, SAD–S, SAR, or SAO) should be embarked on the controlling AGC and the relief AGC. They should disembark after the close of operations one day and be ready to assume

control on a thoroughly tested shore-based set-up early the following morning. Lost motion was noted particularly during the Iwo Jima operation in that when the LFASCU attempted to assume control of troop support missions that they did not have the complete current lists of air liaison parties' requests. After this hiatus was closed, however, the LFASCU did an excellent piece of work and in many cases gave the troops much more nearly what they wanted than was ever possible before the inception of this system.

A new method of coordinating artillery fire and air strikes was used successfully for the first time during this operation. A brief of each air strike was broadcast over the Corps Artillery Fire Direction Control net. Each air strike was given a number and the following information was given: Time bracket, target area, direction of approach and retirement, number and type of aircraft, minimum altitude and any other pertinent information. Each battery of artillery was able to control its fire so as not to interfere with strikes, but a complete shut-down of artillery was only necessary once or twice to run a treetop level Napalm attack. Whenever two or more battalions of artillery were firing on the same target, that information was passed to CASCU with the maximum ordinate and aircraft were warned to keep clear. This proved a very satis factory method of coordination from the air support viewpoint and it is believed to be satisfactory from the artillery viewpoint.

Coordination with naval gunfire still can only be obtained (after fire support has been turned over to the shore fire control parties) by placing "Plan Victor" (limit of maximum ordinate at 1,200 feet) in effect, thus imposing a minimum altitude limitation on the air strike. Fortunately naval gunfire ordinates at the ranges most commonly used are below 1,200 feet and "Plan Victor" does not impose a serious limitation. But the minimum altitude restriction on the air strike places a considerable limitation on the aircraft since bombing and strafing accuracy is greatly increased with decrease in dropping and firing altitude.

In general, communications were excellent on all air support nets on the flagship of TF 53. This ASCU played an important role in maintaining, by relay, communications between other air support participants. On several occasions this unit assumed complete control of various nets during periods of matériel failure in other units. At night considerable CW interference reduced the efficiency of the high-frequency circuits. Numerous instances still exist of aircraft and other stations using the improper net, and of not maintaining good radio discipline on the correct net. Air liaison parties showed evidence on numerous occasions of not being familiar enough with their radio equipment. Both carrier and target antisubmarine patrol being on the same frequency was the cause of considerable interference.

RECOMMENDATIONS

This ASCU was composed of 15 officers and acted as a relief team during the Iwo Jima operation. Considerable difficulty was experienced in adequately monitoring all nets, and still having officers available to relieve others for meals, etc. From this experience, it is felt strongly that the minimum number of officers that a complete operating Air Support Control Unit can function with is 19. Seventeen of these are required for the operating team, including net control officers, communications officers and intelligence officers. Once trained, this team is an intradependent, cooperating unit which cannot afford to have any member on call to any outside source. All planning and over-all jurisdiction of operations must be done by officers who are not a part of the operating team itself. The organization of new strikes, formation of plans for the following day, changes in existing plans and other strategic problems must be worked out by officers who are intimately familiar with, but not involved in, the working of the operating team itself. The planning staff is composed of the ComASCU and the planning officer and is required in the ASCU on the flagship having control of an amphibious operation. No planning staff is required on relief flagships unless it is contemplated that they assume control without being able to transfer any officers from the controlling ASCU.

From: Commander Task Unit 52.2.5 (Commander Carrier Division Seven)

The night carrier mission was primarily to protect the occupation force on Iwo Jima, and its surface support units, from enemy air attack at night. The secondary mission was the daily dusk observation and neutralization of Susaki Airfield, Chichi Jima, the enemy's only nearby airfield from which an attack could be staged against Iwo Jima. (See photographs in pt. IV.) In the event of an enemy surface effort to relieve the hard-pressed Iwo Jima garrison, the destruction of such surface units would immediately become the primary mission of the night carrier group, in conjunction with the day-operating CVE's of the Air Support Group.

To accomplish the mission set forth above the night carrier duties involved:

Night CAP over Iwo Jima, relieved on station.
Special dusk CAP over Iwo Jima.
Daily dusk strikes, and occasional dawn sweeps on Susaki Field, Chichi Jima, with harassing of Haha Jima facilities on return.
Day and night CAP over Task Unit.
Occasional rescue searches.

From the nature of these duties it will be seen that the *Enterprise* maintained a continuous 24-hour air-operations schedule during a large part of this period.

The pilots flying target night CAP over Iwo Jima complained that the VHF channel Dog was very crowded, especially during the early evening hours of the first days of the occupation. Some confusion on the part of the amphibious FDO was evidenced by the large humber of interceptions of friendly surface contacts, largely on occasions when the screen became saturated. As the operation progressed, however, fighter direction at Iwo Jima soon became more efficient though no "splashes" were achieved.

From: Commanding Officer U. S. S. "Petrof Bay" (CVE 80)

There were also instances where the squadron support groups commenced runs on a target designated by CASCU only to find another strike coming in on the same target area from an opposite direction. This situation may have been due to the fact that some support groups were left under the control of their own flight leaders while other groups were controlled by the air coordinator.

NAPALM BOMBS

From Commanding Officer U. S. S. "Randolph" (CV–15)

Bombs and fuzes used by *Randolph* aircraft functioned without any known deficiencies. Napalm bombs were a distinct exception, the estimated observed functioning being from 30 to 50 percent of those dropped. A part of the difficulties may be attributed to the rocky nature of the terrain at Iwo Jima, the only place where Napalm bombs were used.

From: Commander Task Group 51.17, Commander Task Group 51.26 and Commander Task Unit 52.2.3 (Commander Carrier Division Twenty-five)

Replacement pilots received during the operation were so inexperienced that they could not be used as replacements. All were returned to Guam for what is hoped to be a refresher period. With their present training and experience these pilots are of no value as replacements and only take up critical living space aboard ship. It is again recommended that this matter be corrected.

From: Commander Task Unit 52.2.1 (Commander Carrier Division Twenty-six)

The limiting factor in the endurance of CVE's furnishing direct support during a landing operation was proven to be aircraft bombs and rockets. When the operation progressed beyond Dog-plus-Ten-day, ships of this unit were depleted of all aircraft armament except a very few 500-pound SAP bombs and their original number of depth charges. A jury rig pick-up and delivery service of aircraft rockets by a destroyer of the screen was inaugurated but this was slow and painful replenishment, and did nothing to alleviate the destitution of bombs.

From: Commanding Officer U. S. S. "Natoma Bay" (CVE 62)

Innumerable criticisms of radio discipline have been written with no marked improvement. The root of the trouble apparently lies in the fact that VHF transmissions are considered secure, that there is absolutely no reluctance to make unnecessary transmissions, and that there is far too much traffic assigned to four channels (the ton channel VHF should correct this latter complaint. Ships and planes alike are offenders on all counts.

On support missions the support planes should have a free channel, particularly where timed close support missions are in progress. Under these circumstances a sample of the traffic heard while trying to organize a strike is given:

Squeeky this is Wally. Damn it you have been high and fast on the last three passes. Now come down and slow her up.

Number two you are lagging way behind Get in here and stay with me.

Gadget Two this is Gadget Base. Prep Charlie. Over.

Gadget Two this is Gamecock Ten. Prep Charlie. Acknowledge. Over.

Gadget Two this is Gadget Two Three. Gamecock Ten is calling you on channel ten for Prep Charlie.

Hell Gamecock Ten this is Gadget Two. Sorry, I was still on CAP circuit. I am on channel one now. Besides I am in the traffic pattern now. Wilco. Out.

Chapter IV. INTELLIGENCE

From: Commander Amphibious Forces, United States Pacific Fleet (Commander Joint Expeditionary Force)

Intelligence planning and preparation of material for the operation against Iwo Jima presented no unusual problems and followed in general the procedure developed during the preceding three operations participated in by this force. Photographic coverage was unusually good, both in quality and quantity. Early receipt of photographs permitted ample time for the preparation of Intelligence material based on photography. An unusually large amount of this material was prepared and issued. In addition to the frequent photographic coverage of Iwo Jima, an excellent submarine reconnaissance was made by the U. S. S. *Spearfish*. The periscope photography, a sound recording of the actual observations by the sub commander, and soundings taken proved of great value and usefulness.

Previously captured documents and charts provided early and fairly accurate information on terrain, surrounding sea areas, and enemy troop strength. In spite of the unusual amount of advance material it was impossible to accurately determine the exact strength and magnitude of the defensive installations. This was due to the nature of the terrain, effective camouflage, and the fact that the greater part of the defensive installations had been prepared a considerable time before the invasion and had much natural cover. Many of the pillboxes, underground shelters, and entrances to caves had old vegetation growing on and around them.

Air target folders were prepared by ComPhibGrp One and ComAirPac for use by aviators on air support missions, air spotters and observers, and fire support units. These were contact photos with grid and target area shown. On the back of each photo was printed the map of the same area covered by the next photo. These were all bound in a folder, 8 by 8 inches with a cover showing the outline of the various sheets. An aviator looking at the gridded photo, could look at the map (1:10,000) of the same area printed on the back of the sheet he has turned up. These target folders were excellent and most useful. On an island of this size it was possible to do this, but where large areas are to be covered, it will only be practicable to cover the landing area. These folders were distributed separately on a special distribution.

By means of requests to CominCh via CinCPOA, the Atlantic Amphibious Training Command constructed 60 rubber relief models, scale 1:10,000, for use by ships and units of this force. In addition, 40 were constructed for the troops. These models were accurate, and of great value especially to the fire support ships. They were based on the latest and best information available. Ground forms were shown as depicted on the 1:20,000 topographical map.

The organization of four Mobile Hydrographic Units was authorized by the Chief of Naval Operations on 2 December 1943. These units were conceived and organized for the purpose of making rapid advance surveys during assault operations and to perform other functions of immediate importance to the assault units. If considered necessary a final detailed survey is made by a standard naval AGS type of survey ship after capture of the objective.

During the assault on Iwo Jima only two of the four survey vessels were assigned survey duties. The other two continued on screening and patrol work. Hydrographic conditions at Iwo Jima were found to conform closely with those shown on H. O. Chart 6101 and no comprehensive survey program was undertaken. The survey work was confined to searches for reported shoals in the southeastern anchorage area; to the establishment of navigational lights ashore; and some sounding in the mooring buoy area and off Purple and Brown Two western landing beaches.

It is felt that the Mobile Survey Units are of great value in amphibious operations and that their value will be increased as more involved operation areas are encountered.

The amount of captured material examined was limited and did not measure up to the comparative amounts from previous operations. This is contributed to several reasons:

(a) Result of strict orders that no material or documents were to fall in our hands.

(b) The number of caves and pillboxes closed by gunfire.

(c) The slow progress of the advance across the island allowing sufficient time for the destruction of documents of value.

However, all material and documents that were captured were immediately screened for those of immediate value. These were translated on the spot. Those documents of immediate naval interest were sent directly to this command or CTF 53 for translation and use. Others of possible interest were forwarded on to JICPOA.

The planning and execution of public relations arrangements for this operation were on a greatly increased scale over previous operations. A public relations officer was appointed to the Staff for the first time, functioning as a part of the Intelligence Division. CinCPac assigned public relations officers to the *Estes*, the *Auburn* and the *Hamlin*, and temporarily sent a public relations officer to Saipan to facilitate the assignment and reporting of a number of correspondents who joined the force at that port.

The number of correspondents directly assigned to ships of the amphibious force totaled approximately 30, including 4 radio correspondents. The 3 American press associations and Reuters were represented aboard the flagship as were 2 radio correspondents (CBS) representing the combined networks. Many of the leading newspapers and magazines of the country sent individual representatives.

From: Commander Task Group 52.2 (Commander Escort Carrier Force Pacific)

The daily summaries promulgated each day by the Commander Joint Expeditionary Forces (CTF 51) were avidly read and had a decided effect on morale. They are read by all officers engaged in planning or briefing and are paraphrased for all hands. Radio Tokyo's flamboyant and ridiculous broadcasts when compared with the true picture of the progress of battle as described by these summaries gives everyone a good laugh. It is hoped that both stations will continue their news releases.

From: Commander Amphibious Forces, United States Pacific Fleet (Commander Joint Expeditionary Force)

No man-made obstacles were encountered at the water's edge of the beaches as had been found in previous operations, and this is attributed to the fact that they would not have remained in place. The shifting volcanic sand and surf would have soon covered them up or washed them away. However, the natural terraces immediately behind the beaches offered a greater barrier than man-made obstacles. Only tracked vehicles could cross them, and even some of these were stalled by craters in the sides of these terraces. Another reason was that all beaches could be well covered by fire from the Suribachi Mountain to the south, and the high cliffs overlooking the beaches from the north.

The defense inland was the best yet encountered by this force. In spite of the unusual amount of advance information and the excellent large scale photo coverage of Iwo Jima, it was impossible to accurately determine the exact strength and magnitude of the defensive installation. A great majority of the installations were located and printed on the final installation map. Those that were not located could not be located from photographs. This is attributable to the most effective camouflage, both natural and artificial, and the fact that many of the defenses were in caves which were most difficult to locate.

The salient features of the defensive installations were the unusually large number of intricate, heavily protected, interconnected series of underground shelters; an unprecedented number of heavy mutually supporting pillboxes; skillfully placed artillery, mortars, and antiaircraft guns; extensive and effective use of land mines, including those improvised from artillery shells and bombs; and the considerable number of caves in the mountainous and cliff areas which housed supplies, command posts, and artillery, machine guns, and coast defense guns. A good example of the cave system found on the island was found in TA 183L. There were nine entrances to the cave, and the main passageway extended about 800 yards coming out at Minami Village. Two CP's and an aid station had been located there. Many of the above were picked up by aerial photography, but as stated before due to the excellent camouflage and vegetation it was impossible to locate them all. Too, the extent and exact nature was estimated, but no definite information was available. As the operation progressed and vegetation was blasted away, these additional ones were located. However, in the case of many mortar positions, they were not actually located until troops had stepped into them or noted them in passing.

Many of these installations could not be knocked out by air, artillery, or naval gunfire due to their nature and location. These had to be subjected by the troops. Considerable difficulty was experienced with the coast defense guns, all of which were in the caves along the cliffs and on the slopes of Suribachi. Several of the ships of this force sustained serious damage from these guns.

The only water mines found were two moored mines off Blue Beach in approximately 8 fathoms of water. These were destroyed prior to D-day. Several horned mines, 3 to 4 feet in diameter were found floating at sea and destroyed by gunfire or sunk. These were all moss covered and rusty indicating they were old.

Beach mines were found along the first terrace behind the Green and Red Beaches. These were placed 4 feet apart in rows. One small field was found on the western beach just south of Purple Beach. A considerable number of minefields were reported further inland by the troops.

As a whole, this was the best defended, most well organized, and most difficult objective this force has ever operated against. The location and organization of the defenses was the best tactically yet encountered.

Plans for the operation called for the assignment of an experienced oceanographer to the Underwater Demolition Group, in order that preliminary surf observations could be made at the time of the beach reconnaissance; and that forecasts could be made daily of expected surf conditions in conjunction with the aerological officer. Unfortunately, the oceanographer assigned was evacuated to the rear area due to illness just prior to departure of the Underwater Demolition Group for the objective, and no replacement was available.

Aerial observations of the beach conditions, including surf, were made by three observers specially trained for this work. All three were aerological officers who had had a short course in

study of waves and surf at Scripps Institution of Oceanography; special training in aerial observation; and previous experience in the Palau operation. Their reports, as regards surf, were of little assistance in forecasting. The probable reasons for this are, (1) the sea was relatively calm when the observation flights were made, so that the surf was negligible; (2) the character of the beach was such that only a general idea of the surf could be obtained by an aerial view.

The scarcity of reports, and uncertainty of the analysis of the weather map in this area made accurate and dependable forecasts of swell impossible. Within the limits of the weather map, however, such forecasts were made, and the aerological officer on the Attack Force Commander's Staff kept beachmasters and landing forces advised of expected surf conditions.

From: Commander Task Group 51.1 (Commander Transport Squadron 11 and Commander Transport Division 31)

An examination of the excellent beach intelligence photographs available indicated that, if either chop or moderate swell existed LCM and LCVP would, though manned by experienced personnel, be of limited use. The abrupt steep gradient type of beach causes high surf which will poop boats, although skillful handling may prevent broaching.

MAGNETIC PROPERTIES OF SAND ON IWO JIMA

From: A Report by the Military Geology Unit, United States Geological Survey— Giving Results of a Test of a Sample of Beach Sand

This is a clean, course, dark-colored sand.

About 40 percent of the grains are picked up with a strong (Alnico) hand magnet.

Almost all grains are of the same material and composed of varying proportions of the following:

1. Dark brown glass (about one-half to two-thirds).

2. Andesine crystals (about one-quarter to one-third). A few grains have idiomorphic boundaries. All include glass, some an extraordinary large amount. Some grains have a very peculiar scalloped outline.

3. Augite (about one-eighth).

4. Magnetite (accessory grains). Rather abundant in fairly large grains (none occur as dust-like grains). Magnetite gives the sand its strong magnetic property.

5. Ilemnite. A very few grains of ilmenite are included in the magnetite.

In addition to the material described above a few sand grains of a different character are found, namely, a very fine-grained glass andesite with the plagioclase present as microliths. These grains are better rounded than the rest of the material and have clearly been transported farther than the bulk of the material which probably came from the immediate vicinity of the beach.

Conclusion: The magnetite in the rock is the cause of the difficulty encountered in using the SCR–625 land mine detector.

Chapter V. SHIP-TO-SHORE MOVEMENT

From: Commander Amphibious Forces, United States Pacific Fleet (Commander Joint Expeditionary Force)

UNDERWATER DEMOLITION TEAM BEACH RECONNAISSANCE

The reconnaissance of the eastern beaches was conducted by elements of all four UDT's on the morning of Dog-minus-Two. Seven operating platoons were assigned, each of which was responsible for 500 yards of beach. In addition, four standby platoons were designated and in readiness to render assistance or as replacements. Roger-Hour (the time at which the LCP(R)'s carrying team personnel passed the line of LCI(G) support craft) was designated as 1100.

(a) Fire support was furnished by one LCI(G) and one destroyer in close support of each operating platoon. Five additional LCI(G)'s were stationed in reserve positions, and battleships, cruisers, and additional destroyers delivered continuous area coverage in rear of the beaches.

(b) The beach reconnaissance was completed by UDT personnel in accordance with plan. Swimmers were launched from LCP(R)'s at the 500-yard line, and then proceeded in pairs as close to the water's edge as enemy opposition permitted. Reconnaissance was completed and personnel recovered by LCP(R)'s by 1240. During this period the personnel encountered heavier mortar and small arms fire than has been encountered in any previous operation to date. In spite of this fact, only one man was lost during the reconnaissance.

(c) During the reconnaissance the LCI(G)'s in close support moved in to 1,000 yards, where they immediately began to receive effective fire from enemy mortars and fixed artillery. The personnel of these gunboats returned fire with all weapons and refused to move out until they were forced to do so by matériel and personnel casualties. Even then some returned to their stations until

again hit. Relief gunboats replaced damaged ships without hesitation. Between 1200 (K) and 1145 (K) 12 LCI(G)'s had been hit. The exact source of the enemy fire could not be determined and it was decided to direct planes to lay a smoke screen along the beach line. For some reason, as yet unexplained, the smoker planes called for by the OpPlan were not on station, so fire support ships were directed to fire white phosphorous along the beach line 1,000 yards inland from the water's edge and on the flanks. The resultant screen was thin, but was apparently effective in reducing the precision of the enemy fire. As it was noted that little enemy fire was being received beyond 1,800 yards out, destroyers in close support were directed to move in to 2,000 yards from the beach. Their rate of fire at suspected and known targets was intensified and the withdrawal of team personnel was covered. During this period the destroyer *Leutze* was slightly damaged.

The heavy enemy fire drawn by the LCI(G)'s during the reconnaissance of the preferred beaches was not again seen until Dog-Day, although minesweepers and destroyers thereafter and previously came well within range. This lends some support to the conclusion that the Japanese again followed their apparent tendency to hold fire until faced with an actual assault. The approach of 12 LCI craft, which could conceivably carry 2,400 assault troops, preceded by a number of LCP(R), and the fact (known only to the enemy) that the beach profile on the eastern beaches favored the use of large landing craft, would give strength to a belief that an assault was being made. It is therefore recommended that future schemes of maneuver and approach should avoid as much as possible the pattern and suggestion of an assault. In the same vein, UDT personnel in boats should not fire on the beaches except in self defense.

The screen of white phosphorous projectiles on both beaches was of unquestioned value in hampering enemy observation, and reducing the precision of direct fire. The smoke similarly hampered our own fire support, but to a lesser degree because of the inability to definitely locate the enemy installations.

It was originally believed that the use of smoke would result in reduced visibility which would seriously hamper the recovery of swimmers. The team captains unanimously reported that their visibility was never reduced below 100 to 200 yards, and that the light smoke provided a screen for their actions without materially affecting the actions of either the LCP(R)'s or the swimmers.

From: Commander Amphibious Group One (Commander Amphibious Support Force)

It is worthy of note that the defenders did not employ heavy guns against minesweepers even when they worked close to the shore. Perhaps this was because the Japanese knew there were no mine fields to defend and considered that damage to minesweepers would not compensate for disclosure of batteries to the fire support ships. When, however, the LCI(G)'s approached the beach in support of the UDT's, it was logical for the Japanese to assume that being landing craft, they were being employed to carry and land troops. The Japanese therefore opened up with everything they had to defeat the supposed landing. It is therefore considered that LCI(G)'s or craft of that general type should not be used to support UDT's working in the vicinity of strongly defended positions, unless the major defenses are assuredly destroyed beforehand, or unless sufficient ammunition is available to permit the same heavy smothering fire as is used in conjunction with an actual landing.

From: Commander Amphibious Forces, United States Pacific Fleet (Commander Joint Expeditionary Force)

CONTROL

The Iwo Jima operation provided the first test of the amphibious forces' newly formed permanent control organization. This organization was established following the Marianas campaign, where it was realized that proper control of the ship-to-shore movement of amphibious craft had become a continuing 24-hour a day task, requiring specially trained control personnel and specially equipped control vessels.

The control organization for the Iwo Jima operation consisted of the Transport Division, Transport Squadron, and Central (Amphibious Group or Force) Control Officers, permanently assigned to the staff of their respective commanders. This organization now parallels the echelons of both the beach party and the shore party. Control officers were embarked in the same ships as their opposite number in the beach and shore party, giving the maximum amount of time for coordination and understanding of each other's problems prior to the landing.

Each control officer was provided with a control vessel (PCE, PCS, PC, or SC) which had been previously equipped with special communication facilities and provided with a control communication team and advisors from the troops. The control vessels were obtained and equipped, and the personnel trained in their specialized duties, well in advance of the operation. As a result, for the first time the task of controlling the ship-to-shore movement, both during the assault and unloading phases, was handled by "professionals." In addition, control equipped craft were provided to the different troop staffs for use as floating command posts.

At the objective the first five assault waves were dispatched as directed by the central control officer, in order to achieve simultaneous landings on all beaches. At the end of that time the two Transport Squadron control officers took control of the dispatching of reserve waves and the furnishing of supplies for the troops as requested by the beach and shore parties, while the central control officer coordinated all control activities.

During the next few days rough sea and weather conditions required that a large part of the activities of the control organization be concerned with salvage of and assistance to landing craft, DUKW's, LVT's and pontoon barges, many of which broached on the beach or drifted out to sea as a result of high winds and heavy seas. All available control vessels were directed to conduct search sweeps in sectors to leeward of Mount Suribachi. It is believed that all personnel were recovered from these drifting craft, but most of the LVT's and DUKW's taken in tow sank before they could be returned. These operations continued until the morning of D-plus-Five, at which time the beaches were suitable for general unloading. At that time the control group was reorganized to permit unloading of each of the three transport squadrons present under the direction of its own control officer.

From: Commander Task Group 51.1 (Commander Transport Squadron 11) (Commander Transport Division 31)

For the attack, PC(S)'s or PC's specially fitted with communication facilities and teams are provided. For the landing of the reserve, the special teams and equipment are gone—recommendation: Assign communication teams with necessary equipment to the staff of the Transport Squadron Commander in reserve, who has the necessary control personnel but no communication teams or special equipment.

From: Commander Amphibious Forces, United States Pacific Fleet (Commander Joint Expeditionary Force)

RADAR NAVIGATIONAL DEVICE

The radar navigational device known as VPR was employed for the first time during the Iwo Jima assault. This device is designed to fix a vessel's position by apparently superimposing the image of a chart upon the face of a PPI scope, as the result of which the ship's position, indicated at the center of the scope, is "fixed" on the chart.

The equipment was installed in all control vessels at Pearl Harbor and control officers, quartermasters, and radiomen of the ships received instruction both in maintaining a fixed station, and in computing speed-time data to enable the control vessel to arrive at a predesignated point off the beach within a minimum of a few seconds. Both operations are essential in control vessel operations.

Since the installation of VPR in both amphibious force and combatant vessels has been authorized, the following observations may prove of assistance to other commands in the future:

Employment

VPR charts and speed-time charts were drafted en route to the staging point and were reproduced on board U. S. S. *Auburn* and distributed to all control craft prior to departure for the objective. All AGC's are being equipped with facilities for reproducing these charts.

The dawn approach to Iwo Jima was made, using VPR entirely for navigating the control vessels to the Line of Departure. Current data was obtained by plotting the VPR track when the ship was dead in the water. Best results were obtained from observations of 15 or more minutes.

The first assault wave was tracked to the beach by radar and VPR with reasonable success. Radar tracking of subsequent waves was not possible due to congestion in the area off the beach as evidenced in the PPI scope.

After D-day, during rescue and salvage operations, VPR was used to determine the ship's position and facilitate return to the assigned control station. This proved especially valuable during hours of darkness when visual fixes were unobtainable.

In summary, this first extensive use of VPR/NMP navigation in an amphibious operation in the Pacific indicated that VPR/NMP assists the control vessels materially in assuming their proper positions on time. It should be pointed out, however, that VPR was not designed to replace other navigational means, but rather to supplement them. The concept of VPR navigation arose from the need for a means by which ships could make a blind navigation approach to a beach under conditions of poor visibility. VPR does accomplish this within the practical bounds of accuracy. That accuracy depends on (1) the adaptability of the radar gear to VPR modification; (2) the precision of the VPR unit itself; and (3) the skill and experience of the radar operator in obtaining fixes.

The heavy defenses of Iwo Jima, which slowed our advance, permitted enemy mortar fire to cover the landing beaches for several days. Consequently, casualties to beach parties were extremely high—about 60 percent. Elimination of hidden enemy mortar positions is a problem confronting the troops and gunfire support ships; the best protection available to beach party personnel is the knowledge of how to defend themselves by the use of arms, digging of slit trenches, etc. Such combat training is already being provided in some measure to beach parties, but this training must be emphasized and implemented to insure that naval beach party personnel are as well prepared to take care of themselves as are combat troops.

SHORE PARTIES

The composition of the shore party organization had the following disadvantage—many of the personnel were assigned from replacement combat troops of the various troop divisions engaged in the landing and were soon called upon for combat duty prior to arrival of the garrison shore parties. Furthermore, replacement troops received no training whatsoever in shore party duties. This is highly undesirable from both the military and naval standpoint, in that a withdrawal of these combat troops from the unloading organization causes an almost complete cessation of unloading at the beaches, and a consequent serious lack of supplies for the troops ashore, as well as a delay in the withdrawal of transports from the objective, and delay in landing garrison equipment and supplies. It is again recommended that the troop unloading organization be a permanent group especially trained for that task and not subject to withdrawal for other duty except in case of extreme urgency.

From: Commanding General, Headquarters Fourth Marine Division

It is recommended that a permanent organization of size and composition adequate to furnish the basic elements of a Division Shore Party be authorized each Marine Division. The present Pioneer Battalion meets neither of these requirements. A suggested organization to meet the minimum requirements in keeping with the above recommendation is a small Shore Party Regiment consisting of a Headquarters and Service Company and two Pioneer Battalions. The composition of each battalion in both equipment and personnel should be similar to those of the present Pioneer Battalion. Headquarters and Service Company of the regiment should be similar in organization to that of the Headquarters and Service Company of the present Pioneer Battalion.

From: Commander Amphibious Group Two (CTF 53) and (CTG 51.21)

The shore party problem is without question one of the most important and the toughest problems connected with amphibious operations. Its commander must be an extremely capable, forceful and resourceful officer with great organizational ability.

Although the initial assault requirements must necessarily be on call from the separate divisions, it is believed desirable that the Corps shore party assume control from the outset in order to provide the necessary coordination of the supply problem. As at both Saipan and Iwo Jima, difficulties may be experienced on one group of beaches and the entire supply for all troops ashore routed over only one or two beaches. The Corps shore party should be a permanently and separately organized force not subject to the call of any division commander for combat purposes. During this operation the division shore parties were made up largely of replacement troops for the division. This worked fine for a short period but these replacements were soon called up by their division commander, and ultimately resulted in undesirable delays in beach and dump unloading.

All units arrived on schedule and it was apparent as early as 0700 (K) that How-Hour would be met. The only departure found necessary from prearranged plans was the deletion of LCI(G)'s from participation in assault as a result of heavy damage suffered on Dog-minus-Two-Day. The remaining 12 LCS(L)'s rearranged their formation so as to bring all beaches under fire. All preliminary landing preparations proceeded exactly as scheduled. The *Gunston Hall*, carrying LCT's with tanks embarked, completed launching of her three LCT's at 0740 (K). By 0810 (K) all LST's carrying assault troops had been launched.

All air support units arrived on stations promptly. At 0805 (K) naval gunfire was lifted to permit bombing, rocket, and Napalm attacks on landing beaches and beach flanks, and resumed again at 0825 (K).

No gunfire was received in or near transport or LST areas during this period, and transport squadrons were directed to move in 3,000 yards at their discretion.

Assault waves were dispatched on schedule, and landed on all beaches at 0900 (K), the prearranged How-Hour. Only a small amount of gunfire was received in the boat lanes during the approach to the beaches.

The evacuation control LST's launched one pontoon barge each during the morning. These were the only barges launched until Dog-plus-Two-Day. LST's carrying LCT's had previously been ordered to prepare to launch LCT's as soon as LVT's were discharged, and to report readiness. Six of these completed launching prior to sunset, making a total of nine LCT's in the water DOG-night.

LCT's and LSM's carrying tanks were called in to the beach commencing about 0920 (K), and all beached and discharged successfully in spite of enemy gunfire. The tanks, however, encountered great difficulty in moving inland from the beaches. Four LSM's were hit by shellfire while beached but were able to retract under their own power.

TransDiv 32 with one RCT of the Third Marine Division embarked, arrived in the area at 1000 (K). Reembarkation of LVT's in parent LST's commenced at about the same time. Reembarkation continued until early afternoon, at which time all were aboard with the exception of those being used for emergency supply. Loose sand on beaches and heavy enemy fire combined to make unloading of equipment very difficult. Only emergency supplies were landed on Dog-Day. Transports moved in to Area ZEBRA in early afternoon.

During the first day all BLT's of the Fourth and Fifth Marine Divisions, together with half of the division artillery, were landed against increasingly heavy opposition. Initial losses in amphibious vehicles were moderate. No air attacks took place, although unidentified planes caused an alert in the early evening.

Night retirement was conducted in general accordance with previous plans and directives. A total of 11 fire support ships, 7 transport types, and 21 LST's remained at the objective overnight. All LSM's and control craft remained at the objective overnight throughout the operation. No unloading took place during the night, except into LSM's alongside heavy ships remaining at the objective.

BEACH PARTIES

Although operating under unusually difficult conditions at Iwo Jima and under heavy enemy gunfire, it is considered that the coordination between beachmasters and the offshore control vessels was not satisfactory. The following specific points require improvement:

(a) A simplified visual system of calling boats to the beach must be provided. This must include lights for night signalling and range lights for the beaching of larger craft.

(b) A more positive means must be established by control vessels of determining at night what landing craft are in their vicinity waiting for beaching instructions. Particularly during the early phases of assault, night signalling is dangerous and must be kept to a minimum. Radio communication proved only partly satisfactory. On one beach the control officer had an LCPR tender which cruised the area and contacted orally each arriving craft. This proved very satisfactory.

(c) All requests from the troops on shore for materials or supplies must be channelized through the control vessels. In this operation as in preceding ones, there has been a marked tendency for troop commanders to send their requests direct to the ships concerned or to the higher echelons without notification to the control officer and embarked troop representative. This results in loaded craft arriving at the control vessel without any knowledge for their need on the part of the control officer.

The beach condition at Iwo Jima stressed the weakness of our present beach party organization. Practically all members of the beach parties were engaged in their first combat experience. The beach conditions were unusually tough and would have challenged the resourcefulness and efficiency of the most highly trained organization. Successful beach operation under these conditions is an extremely difficult task and it is believed essential that permanent organizations be set up to handle this problem.

Initially it is recommended that a small group of key beach party personnel be constituted and trained in all angles of rough water work and that during an operation they be placed in complete charge of the beaches, supplemented by the required personnel of existing beach parties now aboard transports. Ultimately an organization should be built up corresponding more or less to that of the underwater demolition teams. Such an organization would become highly skilled in beach party work, and would develop a high morale and esprit de corps which is now definitely lacking in beach party organizations. When an operation was in prospect, beach party units could be designated for each beach from this organization. During an operation these beach parties would remain in control of the beaches until such time as the garrison forces took over, thereby eliminating the confusion and inefficiency now existing at that period resulting from beach parties being withdrawn when their ships leave.

From: Commander Transport Squadron Sixteen

At the time the Squadron Beachmaster landed, all beaches were under continuous enemy mortar, artillery, and small arms fire. Fire on Red One, however, was not as heavy as on the other two beaches. Red One was therefore the best beach at the time over which supplies could be delivered. "Priority Cargo" was called for and unloaded by hand at the water's edge wherever a place not under water could be found along the narrow beach strip.

Before the Shore Party could get the cargo up over the terrace or install exits, make cut-throughs, lay matting, and establish roadways, to do so, the beach strip became piled and jammed with various types of cargo due to the fact that it was the best beach and "Priority Cargo" was being rapidly landed in response to demands. For a time, in addition to its own share, Beach Red One was not only receiving cargo which would normally be distributed between the three beaches but it was also receiving cargo destined for the support of the Fourth Marine Division as well as the Fifth Marine Division, due to the impossibility of working Yellow and Blue Beaches. During D-Night, and part of D-plus-1-Day, a large portion of the ammunition received had to be packed up to the lines by hand because sufficient LVT's were not available.

One factor which tended toward confusion in unloading and delay in getting boats into and off the beach was the frequent and everchanging demands for priority cargoes. In many instances, before boats loaded with requested priority cargoes could be landed and unloaded, the priority had changed to another type of cargo. This was due to the fact that BLT Commanders, Beachmasters, and Control Officers were by-passing both the Shore Party Commander, and the Logistics Officer in ordering supplies to the beach.

(a) Early delay in unloading was caused by landing craft of all types retracting to avoid enemy fire and by personnel also seeking cover from enemy fire, air raids, etc.

This, however, was partially corrected by the issuance of specific orders that no type of landing craft, once it had reached the beach, was to retract until it had been completely unloaded and that unloading was to continue regardless of air raids.

(b) Additional delays were caused by cranes, dozers, and tractors sinking into the sand or breaking down and necessitating additional equipment to pull them clear. In addition it was necessary to tow self-propelled vehicles across the beach strip. Even DUKW's had to be towed to the second terrace. In many cases, heavy vehicles required two or three dozers or tractors in tandem to get them across the beach. Failure to unload LVT's at the dumps promptly caused delay in their availability at landing craft waiting to be unloaded. Additional delay which became accumulative and of considerable importance over a period of time was caused by the repeated interruptions of operations by sniper fire and the time lost in rounding up personnel to resume work after its cessation. Another factor was the greatly diminished shore party personnel available at night and the difficulty of keeping such working parties intact.

(c) Night unloading was also hampered somewhat during the early phase by the stationing of LVT(A)'s along the beach at sunset for defense purposes against counter-attack.

(d) Later considerable delay in unloading LCT's was caused by the necessity of the LCT's retracting repeatedly in order to obtain new footing as a result of being carried down on obstructions. In addition, small boats in a number of instances were badly loaded with pallets athwartships, cargo nets overloaded, etc.

From: Commander Task Unit 53.4.1 (Commander LSM Group Thirteen)

A northeasterly wind of about 6 knots and a moderate sea on D-day were favorable for landing on the eastern beaches. The combination of intense enemy fire and the steep beach gradient broached and wrecked numerous LVT's, LCVP's, and LCM's at the surf line. When the LSM's beached, it was difficult to spot a beaching location where the surf line and the beach beyond were clear. The beach and shore parties were dug in right down to the waters edge, which caused further congestion. All six tank loaded LSM's discharged their cargoes rapidly and thereby avoided casualties from enemy fire while on the beaches.

The shore party LSM's which, by the nature of the vehicles and equipment carried required more time to unload, suffered several personnel casualties because of the longer period on the beaches. These LSM's were ordered to beach by the control vessels but were ordered to retract by the beach party before any appreciable unloading had been completed. This occurred not only on the initial beaching but on some of the subsequent beachings before these LSM's had completely discharged their preload. It is believed that if the equipment was not wanted on the beach at the time, the beachmaster should have so informed the control vessels which could have held the

LSM's at the line of departure until they were needed. The control vessels in some instances directed these LSM's to beach on certain beaches, and the LSM's after beaching, were ordered by the beachmaster to retract and land on some other beach.

The LSD's and ARL's performed great service for LSM's and enabled the ships to continue operations and in some cases to remain afloat. The *Belle Grove*, LSD *2* was kept filled with one LSM after another, replacing screws and repairing underwater damage. Damage above the water line and engineering casualties were repaired by the ARL's. As stated above transports assisted in repairing ships alongside when possible. Without the above repair facilities it is doubtful whether more than half of the LSM's could have carried through the unloading phase, and it is quite possible that some might have been lost had they been ordered to continue operating without repairs.

Landing Craft Waves Approaching Beach Under Cover of Naval Bombardment, D-Day (H-Hour-minus-15).

First Five Waves Moving into Beach, D-Day (H-Hour-Minus-6).

Initial Waves Approaching Southeastern Beaches—Note Preinvasion Bombardment, D-Day (H-Hour-Minus).

Enemy Mortar Shells Bursting at Shoreline, Blue Beaches, D-Day.

Troops Preparing to Advance Across Beach Yellow 1, D-Day

*D-Day Afternoon—Note Broached LCVP's Blocking Beach.   Tanks Moving Up Over Rough Sand.
Supplies Beginning To Congest Beach Due to Steep Terraces.*

Chapter VI. LOGISTICS

From: Commander Amphibious Group Two
(CTF 53 and CTG 51.21)

A careful study was made of both the eastern and western beaches of Iwo Jima and plans were prepared for the landing on either side as the weather might dictate. It was apparent that the beaches and beach areas were of extremely soft and shifting sand, which, coupled with their steep gradient and high banks just inshore, indicated that considerable difficulty would be experienced in landing vehicles.

In anticipation of this trouble a large number of runner sleds were provided. In addition the shore party developed and tested a means of hinging marston matting and assembled it in 50-foot units "accordion pleated." Altogether more than 8 miles of this matting were prepared and loaded on sleds in such a manner as to make it available for quick use on the beaches. This proved to be a lifesaver and was responsible to a large degree for the early rapid supply of assault requirements.

At the beach our troubles began. Many of the LVT's and LVT(A)'s temporarily bogged down in the soft sand and were swamped by a steep, quick-breaking single line of breakers about 4 feet high. Some tanks stripped their tracks while trying to make a turn in this soft sand after debarkation from LSM's. LCVP's and LCM's, although beaching initially without difficulty, were swamped either by a large wave breaking over their sterns or by a heavy backwash of surf rushing in over their ramps. These boats broached and by the end of Dog-Day the beaches were almost completely blocked by various types of craft.

The ordinary salvage facilities provided by LCPR's were completely inadequate to take care of this situation and the subsequent clearing of the beaches was made extremely difficult by the fact that the surf quickly filled these boats with sand and also built a bar of sand around them. (See pictorial record pages 8 and 9.)

SMALL BOAT CONTROL

Having experienced difficulty in previous operations with small boats left in the area at night during the assault period, after parent ships had retired, a Small Craft Group was organized to administer and care for miscellaneous small craft. Boats left in the area by retiring ships were directed to the Small Craft Group Commander for securing and berthing and messing of crews, for which two LST(M)'s were available after Dog-Day. This system proved highly satisfactory and is recommended for future operations.

EVACUATION OF CASUALTIES

The evacuation of casualties during this operation showed a marked improvement over any previous operations of this group. Great care had been taken in thoroughly briefing all medical personnel involved before the operation commenced and in providing special medical equipment such as whole blood, which was used here for the first time. Four LST's were outfitted for use as casualty evacuation ships and a large medical staff placed on board. Shortly after How-Hour these vessels each launched one 3 x 12 barge and secured it alongside and moved to a position close to the control vessel off each regimental beach. Casualties coming from the beach, principally in DUKW's and LVT's, were taken aboard the barge and thence by crane to the LST where they were given early medical treatment and then evacuated to transports by LCVP's. During the operation these four vessels handled an approximate total of 6,136 casualties and unquestionably contributed materially to saving many lives. The *Ozark* (LSV 1) proved her worth in handling of casualties. Prior to the operation extra medical personnel had been placed aboard her and on her departure she evacuated a total of 407 casualties.

The lack of hospital facilities ashore was a source of constant concern because of the possibility of bad weather prohibiting embarkation of casualties. It is recommended that every effort be made, particularly in a situation such as this where no suitable harbor was available, to establish hospital facilities ashore at the earliest practicable time.

Transfer during darkness of casualties from the

evacuation control LST's to designated APA's created difficulties which require further solution. LCVP's used for this purpose in many instances had great difficulty in locating the vessel to which directed. Ships designated to receive casualties should display distinctive light groups for this purpose at all times except when danger of air raid or enemy gunfire exists. Transport Squadron Commanders must take positive steps to assure that evacuation control LST's are kept fully informed regarding the designation of ships allocated for receiving casualties. As a general rule night transfers should be reduced to a minimum.

There were a few instances reported of transports refusing to receive casualties from LCVP's after these craft were given orders by evacuation control officers of LST(H)'s to unload their casualties to these ships. Reasons given were that the transports were overtaxed or were not the ships designated as casualty receivers. This condition must not occur.

The boats returning from the beach during the early stages of the assault were found to be inadequate for the evacuation of casualties from the LST(H)'s to the transports, and it was necessary for the TransRon commanders to detail more boats to each LST(H) for this service.

It is recommended that TransDiv commanders maintain close liaison with their assigned LST(H)'s and assign additional LCVP's as circumstances require.

LSV *Ozark*, serving as an emergency hospital ship during the night and when transports left the objective, rendered invaluable service, and a greater number could well be used in future operations.

Recommend that medical personnel of landing force hospitals and garrison hospitals be temporarily detailed to this type of ship to augment their medical complement until such time as their services are required ashore.

From: *Commanding General Expeditionary Troops* (CTF-56)

HOSPITAL LST's

Four of these ships had been given additional medical personnel, equipment, and supplies to prepare them to receive casualties and act as Evacuation Control Ships. They also had a few structural changes made and carried a pontoon barge for transferring casualties. One of the four had reefer boxes, a flake ice machine and the personnel assigned to operate the blood bank. It was stocked with whole blood and acted as a floating blood bank until the blood bank was established ashore on D-plus-8. All of these ships, however, brought LVT's to the target and were converted for casualty use after these were unloaded.

The design of these ships makes it difficult to care for casualties when empty and after being unloaded they were covered with dirt and grease. The illumination in the tank deck is very poor and the operating facilities are entirely inadequate. The medical personnel assigned to them was not sufficient to care for the very large number of casualties passing through them in spite of heroic effort on their part. On D-day from 0900 to 1530 there had been 1,230 casualties evacuated through these LST's. This was slightly more than three casualties per minute. After a few days and nights of this the medical officers and corpsmen were exhausted.

The barges alongside for transferring casualties were usually violently unstable. At times the barges would rise on the swell to the level of the LST deck and on one occasion the barges had to be cut loose. However, the transfer of casualties to transports from LVT's was equally difficult, if not impossible at times, and some means of transferring casualties from LVT's to LCVP's was needed since the LCVP's could be hoisted on the davits to the deck level of the transport and casualties brought aboard this way. LVT's and DUKW's cannot be hoisted in this manner. It is easier to handle casualties in a DUKW than in an LVT, apparently due to the ease of handling the DUKW in a seaway. It has more freeboard, steers easier, and is very roomy. One LST served one beach and evacuated casualties to its transport division or to the hospital ship. With the establishment of hospitals ashore the LST's were withdrawn and at that time more DUKW's were available to facilitate the movement of casualties seaward.

It is believed that the Evacuation Control LST's served a very useful purpose, but if they are used for the care of casualties they should not be used for anything else and must be adequately staffed and equipped for this very important job. They must also have several structural alterations to allow for easy passage of the casualties from the tank deck to the operating rooms and should have permanent installations for the care of casualties on the tank deck.

Casualties among corpsmen were very high, especially among front line units. In moving about to care for the wounded, they were subject to intense enemy fire and frequently were shot down alongside the man they were caring for. For this operation, each division was assigned approximately 5 percent additional corpsmen before the operation; however, the losses among corpsmen in one Marine Division (4th Mar. Div.) were approximately 38 percent and a little less in the others so that there was need for additional replacements and medical companies were levied on to furnish these. In one division this was carried to such an extent that by D-plus-Eight-Day, one medical company had been reduced to three Medical Officers and a few Marines and was completely inoperative as an organization. This is contrary to established doctrine and greatly hinders the care of the wounded. The hospital sections of the medical companies must not be disrupted to furnish replacements for front line units or there will be no one to care for the wounded after they are evacuated from the front lines.

From: Commander Amphibious Group Two (CTF 53 and CTG 51.21)

SALVAGE ORGANIZATIONS

The rough weather and treacherous beach conditions created a beach salvage problem which far exceeded the capacity of the usual organization set up to handle it.

As our operations progress toward the Japanese homeland, rough weather conditions will generally prevail and immediate steps should be taken to perfect and expand our beach salvage organization.

A special beach salvage group should be organized. Vessels of that group should include small tugs, YTB's, LCI types, and specially equipped LCM's carrying pumps, shallow water diving units, and underwater burning outfit. This organization would be augmented during the assault phase by LCP(L)'s or LCPR's provided by Transport Squadron Commanders for minor salvage work on their own beaches.

In addition to the above, each assault transport should provide a mobile repair unit capable of above-water welding and minor hull and engine repair to landing craft afloat.

PREVENTION OF ALONGSIDE DAMAGE

In the rough sea conditions prevailing at Iwo Jima the LST's, LSM's, LCT's, and smaller craft suffered extensive damage while alongside larger vessels. All available fenders were soon carried away and makeshift fenders proved inadequate. Cane fenders themselves caused considerable damage because of their small pressure area. Mounting lugs for causeways and pontoon barges on the sides of LST's were a particular source of damage to vessels and smaller craft alongside. In future operations it is most important that each large ship and LST be provided with suitable fenders or small camels.

Unloading of assault shipping on Dog-Day and Dog-plus-One-Day was confined to LST's and LSM's, except for a floating reserve of LCVP's and LCM's maintained at each control vessel, loaded with ammunition, water, rations and medical supplies. Surf conditions soon proved it useless to try landing supplies by small boats and by Dog-plus-One-Afternoon all unloading of transports was confined to LCT's and LSM's. APA's and AKA's were restricted to unloading "On Call" from Dog-plus-One to Dog-plus-Five. When shipping availability permits, APA's should carry ammunition, emergency rations, water, medical supplies, and vehicles only. All organizational gear should be loaded on the AKA's. Ordinarily the beach is never ready to receive on Dog-Day anything but this type of cargo. APA's loaded in this manner could completely unload immediately and retire from the area. As other types of supplies are needed and wanted on the beach the AKA's can supply it faster than the beach parties can handle.

The loading into LCT's and LSM's must be more carefully supervised by the commanding officers of transports. Many transports overloaded the smaller craft, or dumped the supplies into them giving no thought to the difficulties of unloading on the beach. In some cases large heavy boxes were loaded on top of an already overloaded LCT causing hours of delay on the beach in unloading.

The preloading of LST's again proved highly satisfactory, the only error being in loading of B rations. The preloaded supplies must be confined to supplies needed on the beach early in the operation.

LSM's should be preloaded with supplies in a

like manner as LST's to take advantage of the tonnage they can carry.

The loading of garrison assault units in assault troop shipping should be discontinued if practicable. Garrison assault units should be loaded in their own ships so they can be unloaded when needed without having to retain several partially loaded assault ships in the area.

Garrison echelons coming into hostile areas prior to the securing of the areas, must be prepared to start unloading immediately on arrival. They must be equipped to take care of themselves. Messing of unloading crews must be arranged for prior to departure. Rear echelons should see that ships of this class are properly prepared and fitted out before they sail. This is especially true when they are part of the assault shipping.

Two resupply ammunition ships had to be called into the area early in the operation. The first ship, *Columbia Victory*, arriving Dog-plus-Six. The ammunition needed was primarily mortar and artillery. The 155-mm. ammunition was all stowed in one hatch and the 105-mm. stowed in two hatches, one of these being the same hatch as the 155-mm. The ammunition needed primarily by the troops being 155-mm. and 105-mm., it meant working only two hatches. This did not allow the ship to be worked at the required rate as if the different types of ammunition had been spread throughout the five hatches. The loading of the *Joliet Victory* was the same as the *Columbia Victory*, with all artillery ammunition in two hatches.

For future operations where the beaching of LST's is possible, it is recommended that LST's be loaded with about 1,000 tons of high priority ammunition. Experience has taught that only three or four types of ammunition is required by the troops in addition to the initial supply. If the LST's are not capable of beaching or unloading at a causeway, larger ships must be loaded so that all priority types of ammunition are available from all hatches.

PONTOON BARGES AND CAUSEWAYS

The difficulty with pontoon barges and causeways have been discussed elsewhere. In future operations the following instructions should govern:

(*a*) They should not be launched in rough sea conditions.

(*b*) If any doubt exists, a few should be launched at a time until operating conditions are definitely determined.

(*c*) Procedure should be developed for assuring that engines are in operating condition prior to launching.

(*d*) A towing bridle should be provided. The sharp edges of pontoon sections quickly chafe through ordinary towing gear.

(*e*) All barges and causeways should have their numbers clearly painted on both sides and on the deck for identification in case of break-down and subsequent salvaging.

(*f*) Plans should prescribe a definite anchorage and beach area for these structures.

From: Commander Task Unit 53.4.2 (Commander LSM Group Fourteen)

On D-day the wind and sea were from the northeast: wind, force 6 knots; sea, slight swell; surf on the beach moderate. The LSM's carrying tanks experienced difficulty in landing their loads because the tanks bogged down off the end of the ramp, blocking the unloading. This necessitated many beachings. Also the wreckage on the beach, plus the marines pinned down at the water's edge left little space to land. These ships encountered severe mortar, artillery, and small arms fire. Later, when the shore party equipment LSM's landed, the beach was almost totally blocked with wrecked LCVP's, LVT's, LCM's, and tanks. These LSM's on first beachings landed only bulldozers and beach-matting; both items were sorely needed. It was impossible for wheeled vehicles to get any traction in the soft sand. Much of the shore party equipment was destroyed shortly after being landed.

The entire port side of all LSM's have been structually weakened with seams split and frames and longitudinals buckled, bent, and broken. All equipment on the port superstructure deck has been damaged or carried away. This includes the 50-caliber and 20-mm. machine guns, ventilators, wherrys, fire fighting equipment, gun tubs, davits, stanchions, life rafts, etc.

The port sides have been pushed in from 6 to 10 inches, buckling decks, breaking piping and wiring, damaging equipment, and springing the watertight doors so that they cannot be closed. Holes were punctured above and below the water line by submerged wreckage, broaching landing craft, and loose pontoon barges.

All propellers were bent or damaged; several stern anchors were lost. Cargo nets fouled the screws of over half the LSM's operating.

It is recommended that adequate camels 40 to 50 feet long and 4 feet wide be used in this type unloading. These would tend to spread the strain of impact over a large area and lessen the damage.

The bough fenders used by the transports smashed huge dents in the sides between the frames.

Too much emphasis cannot be placed on the need for efficient salvage operation and clearing the wreckage off the beaches. The loose causeways and pontoon barges were a deadly hazard and should be kept under control. Moreover, a great effort should be made to keep cargo nets and lines out of the water.

From: Commanding Officer U. S. S. "Fayette" (APA-43)

Palletized cargo, where it can be handled as planned in LCM's and LCVP's has distinct advantages. Unfortunately, several difficulties arose which made it necessary to break the vast majority of pallets on this ship before unloading them. The first difficulty was that the loading plans of the ship did not anticipate pallet loading so a certain amount of the pallets had to be broken in order to get all the cargo on board. The remaining pallets were stowed under and around the squares of the hatches where they could be reached by the cargo hook. The pallets that were loaded into LCM's were handled on the beach quickly and efficiently. However, only a small part of the bulk cargo was unloaded into LCM's. Most of it was loaded into an LST, an LSM, and an LCT. All the pallets loaded into these craft had to be broken and handled by cargo nets, resulting in delays and increased labor.

Cargo or "trip" tickets. The requirement that each net load of cargo be accompanied by a signed mimeographed form filled out in triplicate showing exactly what was in the net, was a source of constant delay and irritation. The plan was to retain one copy on board, deliver one copy to the control officer, and one to the beachmaster. The system finally broke down under its own weight. It is recommended that "trip tickets" be abolished in future operations.

The boat control system was so complex and rigid that boat coxswains had difficulty getting through to discharge their cargo even when all beach conditions were favorable. By the time the coxswain had delivered trip tickets and received orders from the various control officers to "wait" he was very nearly discouraged. When a ship has its own assigned beach, its own beachmaster, its own boat group commander, it is recommended that the boat group commander be allowed to send in his boats as they arrive and beach conditions permit. This is the system that has worked in an efficient, simple, and speedy manner in previous operations.

From: Commanding Officer U. S. S. "Talladega" (APA-208)

The "Hot Cargo" pool of LCVP's while considered an excellent scheme under suitable conditions, did not work out well in this operation due to the nature of the beach and bad surf conditions. A large proportion of cargo loaded into "Hot Cargo" boats had to be loaded back aboard ship and sent ashore in larger craft.

From: Commanding Officer U. S. S. "Sibley" (APA-206)

It was plainly evident that carrying life rafts over the side abreast No. 4 hatch or anywhere else below the main deck level is impractical when handling LSM's or LCT's alongside. These rafts have been removed and stowage found for them inboard clear of the side.

From: Commander Transport Division Forty-five

The value derived from submitting cargo unloading reports every 2 hours is questioned. With few LCT's and LSM's available and the impossibility of discharging cargo on the beaches using ship's boats, the transports often went hours without unloading. The cargo unloading reports in those cases did not change. It is believed that three cargo unloading reports a day would suffice to present an accurate picture. Any reduction in routine reports required will reduce the communication load and permit priority messages getting through more rapidly.

From: Commanding Officer LCT(6) Group 48 (CTU 53.7.5)

UNDERWATER HULL DAMAGE

The amount of underwater damage is best illustrated by the fact that before the assault was over, each LCT had been drydocked in an LSD at least once, five of them twice. The causes were three: First, failure to remove pad-eyes welded on sides of LCT's to secure launching ways; second, submerged wrecks on beach; and third, collisions at beach with other craft. All three combined to produce an unusually large number of holes in voids, patching of which required the cutting away of whole sections of underwater plating. The first cause could easily be eliminated, either by countersinking the pad-eyes, making them removable, or by adding extra plating behind them. The second cause was a natural part of the operation, as was the third. Heavy surf caused ships to swing into one another while on the beach. Holes in the bottom were relatively few, but those in generator rooms caused much trouble. Vibration of generators created cracks in deck. Damage to shafts was not widespread, but there was much operational time lost due to fouled screws, arising from debris on beach. LCT (6) *1154* twice lost its starboard screw due to improper size of shaft. Due to necessity of continuing operations, no attempt to repair ships was made during the first 2 weeks except as ships became inoperable. Repair facilities were inadequate, but only because of the excessive amount of damage suffered. At the end of 2 weeks, extensive repairs were begun and are continuing.

From: Commanding General, Headquarters Fourth Marine Division, Fleet Marine Force

The tactical loading of assault elements in LST's was necessarily different for the Iwo Jima operation than in previous ones in which the division had participated. For the Saipan operation, at least 8 LST's had been provided for each assault RCT, allowing 4 for each assault BLT in which 3 rifle companies, BLT support elements, and a proportional part of the LVT(A)'s were embarked. The LVT(A)'s were distributed equally throughout the 16 LST's assigned assault RCT's. Because of the limited number available to the division for the Iwo Jima operation, only 7 LST's could be allotted to each assault RCT while 5 were assigned to the artillery regiment. Each assault RCT in turn assigned 3 to each assault BLT and embarked the LVT(A)'s of its Armored Amphibian Company in the remaining 1 (a

hospital LST). This plan did not provide equitable distribution of personnel, LST's embarking assault companies being overloaded beyond the capacity limit assigned by higher echelon, particularly those carrying radar and pontoon barge personnel. LST's with armored amphibians were loaded to less than one-third capacity in personnel. It is believed that in the future assignment of LST's for an operation, consideration should be given to recommendations submitted by the division which bases its requirements on the tactical plan, involving the maintenance of tactical unity, rather than upon a mathematical solution arrived at by dividing the number of LVT's and LVT(A)'s to be lifted by the capacity of an LST.

From: Commander Amphibious Forces, United States Pacific Fleet (Commander Joint Expeditionary Forces)

Distribution of troop personnel and matériel

IWO JIMA ASSAULT FORCES

Unit	Officers	Enlisted	Short tons (including vehicles)	MT (including vehicles)	Number of vehicles
Fourth Marine Division:					
APA's–AKA's	1,015	16,601	13,632	32,436	1,194
LST's–LSM's	254	6,582	9,585	28,764	687
Total	1,269	23,183	23,217	61,200	1,881
Fifth Marine Division:					
APA's–AKA's	979	17,271	13,110	36,791	1,221
LST's–LSM's	322	7,216	9,574	30,101	611
LSD	6	90	589	750	18
Total	1,307	24,577	23,273	67,641	1,850
Third Marine Division:					
APA's–AKA's	1,081	17,925	14,155	33,465	1,438
LST's–LSM's	37	497	1,623	2,125	54
LSV	7	50	279	1,241	50
Total	1,125	18,472	16,057	36,831	1,542
Corps (and attached garrison):					
APA's–AKA's	398	4,573	10,425	29,137	1,028
LST's–LSM's	270	5,444	11,818	34,205	1,010
Total	668	10,017	22,243	63,342	2,038
Total assault force	4,369	76,249	84,790	229,014	7,311

Measurement tons per man

Fourth Marine Division	2.50
Fifth Marine Division	2.61
Third Marine Division	1.89
Corps	5.93
Assault force	2.84

STANDARD LST LOAD No. 1

The following articles will be stowed at the after end of the tank deck of each LST receiving this load:

AMMUNITION

No.	Article	Rounds	Boxes	Cube	Weight
					Pounds
1	.30-caliber carbine, M1	90,000	30	30	3,030
2	.30-caliber ball (5 rounds)	61,500	41	61	4,592
3	.30-caliber ball (8 rounds)	72,296	59	88	6,372
4	.30-caliber tracer (8 rounds)	36,000	24	36	2,640
5	.30-caliber AP and tracer (belted 4–1)	152,000	152	134	12,160
6	.45-caliber ball	4,000	2	2	220
7	.50-caliber AP and tracer (belted 2–2–1)	11,340	54	104	4,320
8	12-gauge No. 00 buckshot	1,500	3	3	198
9	37-mm. cannister M–2	140	7	15	714
10	37-mm. HE, N63 w/f BD, M58	260	13	27	1,183
11	37-mm. APC N51, w/tracer	260	13	30	1,300
12	60-mm. mortar, HE M49A2, w/f PD M52	2,872	359	438	18,237
13	75-mm. gun, HE, M48 (SC) A1	147	49	83	3,920
14	75 mm. gun, HE, M48 (NC) w/f PD M54	147	49	83	3,920
15	75-mm. gun, APC M61, M66 A and tracer	369	123	227	9,963
16	81-mm. mortar HE, M43A1, w/f PD, M52	490	82	158	5,986
17	81-mm. mortar, M56	392	196	208	8,310
18	Rocket AT, 2.36″ M6–H3	200	10	33	1,270
19	Grenade, hand, frag. Mk. II w/f N10A3	1,625	65	82	3,705
20	Grenade, adapter, M1	1,008	21	36	922
21	Grenade, adapter, T–2	48	1	2	40
22	Grenade, hand illum	200	8	10	463
23	Grenade, hand inc., frag	48	4	5	180
24	Grenade, rifle, AT M9A1	940	94	94	3,008
25	Cartridge, gren, carbine M6.[1]	(1)	(1)	(1)	(1)
	Total cube and weight			1,769	90,921

Item	Quantity (bbls., cases, etc.)	Cubic feet	Weight
Emergency rations:			*Pounds*
C-rations	100	100	4,500
D-rations	27	27	1,080
K-rations	100	138	2,800
Total	227	265	8,380
Water (5-gallon cans) 4,000 gallons	800	720	44,000
Automatic supplies:			
Toilet paper—1 case (100 rolls)			
Laundry soap—2 cases (120 bars)			
Salt water soap—2 cases (40 bars)			
Wire: 50 rolls, concertina		150	2,750
LVT maintenance:			
Distilled water (5-gallon can)	1	1	50
Rags (2 bales)	2	3	50

[1] One box on each of 2 LST's. Not included in standard load.

2. The following articles will be secured to the main deck as far forward as possible on each LST receiving this load:

Item	Quantity (bbls., cases, etc.)	Cubic feet	Weight
Petroleum:			*Pounds*
Gasoline, 100-octane	20	200	10,000
Gasoline, 80-Octane	20	200	10,000
Cleaning solvent	1	11	500
Gasoline unloaded	1	11	500
Oil (SAE 50, detergent)	5	55	2,500
Oil (SAE 30, detergent)	1	11	500
Grease, No. 2 type (cane)	8	8	572
Rust preventative (drums)	2	22	1,000
Total		518	25,272

3. The following articles will receive special stowage in accordance with current safety regulations as directed by AdComPhibsPac.:

No.	Article	Rounds	Boxes	Cube	Weight
					Pounds
1	2-inch mortar, M3 bomb smoke, M14M2	306	17	19	765
2	60-mm. mortar, illum. M83	320	40	49	2,032
3	60-mm. mortar, smoke, W. P. T6	144	18	22	914
4	60-mm. mortar, smoke, H. C. T8	136	17	21	864
5	75-mm. gun, smoke, W. P. Mk. II	74	25	44	2,019
6	81-mm. mortar, smoke W. P. M57	99	33	56	1,650
7	Rocket AT, smoke W. P.	96	8	19	680
8	Grenade, smoke, H. C. M8	200	8	14	480
9	Grenade, smoke, W. P. M15	850	34	61	2,482
10	Grenade, rifle, smoke, W. P.	40	4	5	144
11	Grenade, hand, colored assorted	150	6	9	288
12	Grenade, colored T8E1 assorted	40	4	4	128
13	Grenade signal colored smoke assorted	100	(1)	(1)	(1)
14	Light signal Very-Gree Star, Red Star, White Star	(2)	(2)	(2)	(2)
15	Signal ground assorted	144	3	7	276
16	Flare trip, M-48	(3)	(3)	(3)	(3)
17	Flare trip, M-49	250	10	18	590

1 Packing unknown.
2 1 box assorted in each of 3 LST's.
3 121 per LST—packing not known.

CASUALTIES SCREENED BY LST(H)'s

Day	Date	LST(H) 929	LST(H) 930	LST(H) 931	LST(H) 1032	Daily total
D-day	19 Feb	281	398	88	218	985
D-plus-1	20 Feb	168	248	249	151	816
D-plus-2	21 Feb	31	230	220	223	704
D-plus-3	22 Feb	26	40	37	118	221
D-plus-4	23 Feb	200	279	46	96	621
D-plus-5	24 Feb	93	309	96	209	707
D-plus-6	25 Feb	26	132	225	56	439
D-plus-7	26 Feb	46	574	226	30	876
D-plus-8	27 Feb	45	324	136	87	592
D-plus-9	28 Feb	0	175	0	0	175
		916	2,709	1,323	1,188	6,136

SUMMARY OF NAVAL BATTLE CASUALTIES

	KIA [1]	WIA [1]	MIA [1]
Transports, Group Able (53.1)	12	19	39
Beach parties, Group Able	0	3	1
Transports, Group Baker (53.2)	3	77	15
Beach parties, Group Baker	4	44	11
Transports, Reserve Group (51.1.1)	4	2	0
Beach parties, Reserve Group	0	0	0
Cruisers	17	120	0
Carriers and support carriers	25	87	362
DD's, APD's, and DMS's	31	55	9
Support planes (CTF 51, 24 planes)	13	4	13
LST's	9	28	0
LSM's	4	30	2
LCT's	2	10	0
Small craft groups	0	1	0
UDT groups	17	22	0
Mortar support groups	0	4	0
Pontoon barge and LCT group	0	1	0
Gunboat support group	17	58	0
Net and buoy unit	17	44	0
Seaplane base group (AV)	0	8	0
Survey ship	1	2	0
Ammo ship	0	1	0
Ditched plane 46V609	0	6	0
Total	176	626	452

[1] Total KIA, WIA, MIA, 1,254.

Day	Date	KIA	WIA	MIA	Cumulative total	Daily total
D-day	19 Feb	76	1,080	5	1,161	1,161
D plus 1	20 Feb	264	1,562	481	3,055	1,894
D plus 2	21 Feb	426	2,116	355	3,969	919
D plus 3 and 4	22, 23 Feb	870	4,711	670	6,251	2,282
D plus 5	24 Feb	1,021	5,284	537	6,845	594
D plus 6	25 Feb	1,195	6,006	549	7,750	905
D plus 7	26 Feb	1,347	6,791	484	8,622	872
D plus 8	27 Feb	1,556	7,984	586	10,126	1,504
D plus 9	28 Feb	1,616	8,418	575	10,661	535
D plus 10	1 Mar	1,845	9,150	599	11,595	934
D plus 11	2 Mar	2,005	9,780	545	12,333	738
D plus 12	3 Mar	2,278	10,632	541	13,451	1,118
D plus 13	4 Mar	2,468	10,556	631	13,655	204
D plus 14	5 Mar	2,620	10,753	546	13,919	264
D plus 15	6 Mar	2,715	11,054	452	14,221	302
D plus 16	7 Mar	2,869	11,505	430	14,804	583
D plus 17	8 Mar	3,055	12,251	435	15,741	937
D plus 18	9 Mar	3,191	12,723	445	16,359	618
D plus 19	10 Mar	3,315	13,203	421	18,204	581
D plus 20	11 Mar	3,488	13,785	419	17,692	752
D plus 21	12 Mar	3,653	14,130	421	18,204	512
D plus 22	13 Mar	3,765	14,403	434	18,692	398
D plus 23	14 Mar	3,878	14,750	434	19,062	460
D plus 24	15 Mar	4,112	15,102	437	19,653	591
D plus 25	16 Mar	4,206	15,290	423	19,928	275
D plus 26	17 Mar	4,305	15,474	417	20,196	268
D plus 27	18 Mar	4,357	15,511	397	20,265	69
D plus 28	19 Mar	4,403	15,598	391	20,392	127
D plus 29	20 Mar	4,457	15,677	359	20,493	101
D plus 30	21 Mar	4,503	15,732	353	20,538	95
D plus 31	22 Mar	4,540	15,820	336	20,696	108
D plus 32	23 Mar	4,590	15,954	301	20,845	149
D plus 33	24 Mar	4,590	15,954	301	20,845	0
D plus 34	25 Mar	4,590	15,954	301	20,845	0
D plus 35	26 Mar	4,590	15,969	301	20,860	15

The Steep Beach Gradient, the Surf, and the Volcanic Sand Caused Numerous Small Craft To Broach— Note Flooding From Backwash Over Ramp.

LST's and LSM's Are Forced To Land Close Together Due to Wreckage and Lack of Exits Over Steep Terrace.

Though Broached, Prompt Action Saved the Supplies.

Unimproved Roads Impeded the Movement of Supplies.

Lack of Exits Caused Congestion of Supplies on Beaches.

Bulldozers Reduced the Terraces Making Exits to the Lateral Roads.

Preassembled Marston Matting on Runner Sleds was Laid on Roads and Beach Exits.

Handling Palletized 105-mm. Ammunition

A General View of RED Beach Showing Matting on Roads.

Unloading of Pontoon Barge With an LVT.

Delivering Cargo on Runner Sleds—Note Casualty Evacuation Station in Background.

Beach and Surf Conditions Wrecked Numerous Barges. Uncollected Cargo Nets on the Beach Went Adrift and Fouled Propellers of Small Craft.

Dog-Day-Plus-Eleven. Opposites With the Same Fate.

The Marston Matting Showed the Effects of Heavy Traffic but the Supplies Were Cleared From the Beaches.

LSD Renders Assistance to a Pontoon Barge.

LCT 1029 Broached on Dog-Day-Plus-Eleven and Eventually Had to Be Sunk at Sea.

Beach Scene, Beach Yellow 2. Wrecked DUKW and AMTRACK—Jap Lugger, D-Plus-2-Day.

Beach Scene, Beaches Green, Red 1 and 2. Note Broached Pontoon Causeways, D-Plus-7-Day.

Slow Unloading—Each Carton of Rations Manhandled Twice. Apparently No Trucks or LVT's Loaded in the LSM, Being Used. Instead Roller Conveyors Are Used.

Little Space To Beach Among the Wreckage. Note the LSM Beach Mat in the Foreground. They Proved Very Beneficial on D-Day.

Wrecked LVT's on Yellow Beach 1, D-Plus-2-Day.

LST's Unloading. Note Marston Matting in Foreground, Beach Red 1, D-Plus-7-Day.

LST's and LSM's Unloading on Green and Red Beaches. Suribachi Mountain in
Background, D-plus-5-Day.

View of Island Looking North.   Unloading on Southeastern Beaches, D-plus-5-Day.

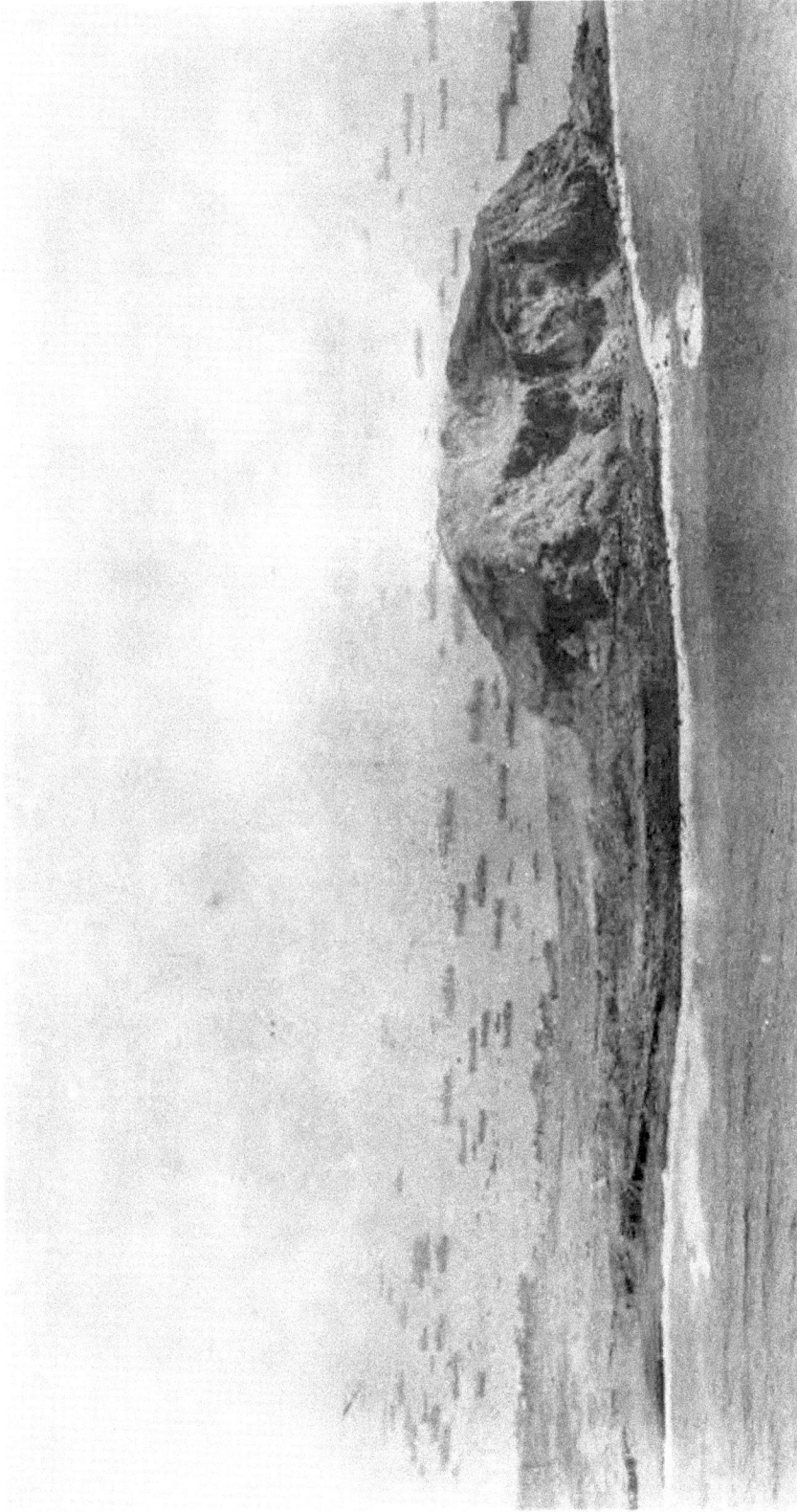

Dog-plus-Five Aerial View of Suribachi and the Transport Area.

The Southern Half of the East Beaches on the Afternoon of Dog-Plus-Five.

CHAPTER VII. MISCELLANEOUS

From: Commander Amphibious Forces, United States Pacific Fleet (Commander Joint Expeditionary Force)

LSV AND LSD's

In addition to the heavy ships, one LSV and three LSD's, all of which were in the forward area, were assigned to the operation. The LSV was assigned to the Third Marine Division and loaded a medical company and 50 amphibious trailers loaded with rations, ammunition and water for emergency use ashore. It was intended that the LSV be employed primarily as a medical evacuation ship. The LSD's were originally intended to transport LCT's and LCM(3)'s loaded with medium tanks from Saipan to the objective. One lot of 18 tanks was to have been distributed among 3 LCT's and the other two lots of 18 tanks in LCM(3)'s. When it was found by tests conducted that the current model medium tank to be used in the operation exceeded the safe loading limit of the LCM(3) it was decided to use 6 LSM's to transport the 36 medium tanks which were to have been loaded in two of the LSD's. The two LSD's were required at the objective to provide small craft docking and repair facilities and accordingly were employed to transport the 36 LCM(3)'s each of which received a substitute load of naval resupply ammunition, 1 lot being loaded at Guam from shore stocks and the other at Saipan from 8 of the LST's carrying preload No. 3 comprising naval resupply ammunition.

LST's AND LSM's

Sixty LST's and twenty-five LSM's were originally available for the operation. Subsequent to issuance of loading orders results of tests confirmed that the medium tanks being used were of greater weight than those previously used and too heavy to be transported in LCM(3)'s loaded in LSD's as intended. Accordingly, six additional LSM's were requested making the final allocation of LST's and LSM's as follows:

	LST's	LSM's
4th MarDiv:		
LVT's	14	--
Halftracks and vehicles	--	3
Medium tanks	--	10
Shore party	--	3
Artillery	5	--
	19	16
5th MarDiv:		
LVT's	14	--
Vehicles and shore party	--	6
Medium tanks	--	6
Artillery	5	--
	19	12
5th PhibCorps:		
Artillery	6	--
Shore party	3	3
AAAW Bn	3	--
Vehicle loaded supplies	2	--
Construction Bn(naval)	2	--
Engineer Bn	2	--
3rd MarDiv tanks	2	--
AAA Bn	2	--
	22	3
Total	60	31

LANDING CRAFT

LCM(3) AND LCV(P)

Landing boats were particularly ineffective during this operation due to the nature of the beaches. The slope at the water's edge was very steep, the black volcanic sand was soft, loose, and more nearly resembled a very light, fine cinder which would not pack, than a sand beach.

When boats were driven up hard onto the beach in an effort to provide a dry ramp and set the boat firmly on the sand, the stern was nearly submerged and in many cases boats were swamped by the surf which broke directly on the beach and into the boat. If the boat was not well beached, waves surging up the steep slope tended to flood the boat through the open ramp. Boats would not hold their positions in the soft sand and there were many broached boats. LCM's were less affected by the beach and surf conditions but both LCM(3) and LCV(P) were continuously in danger of swamping and broaching as long as they remained beached. Once broached, boats were speedily engulfed in the soft sand which made the salvage problem difficult.

As the operation progressed surf conditions became steadily worse; it soon became evident that LCV(P)'s could not negotiate the beaches and they were withdrawn from beach operation. LCM's were used in decreasing numbers until Love-plus-Five when their use was discontinued on eastern beaches. Although the slope of the western beaches was less abrupt than on the eastern beaches, and surf conditions good after unloading in this area began, there was still continuous danger of broaching and it was necessary to run engines in an effort to hold the boats on and give some measure of control.

Stern anchors were not used during the operation, and although they might have prevented broaching in some cases, their use is not recommended under similar circumstances as one of the major difficulties encountered in handling LST's and landing craft on these beaches came from fouled screws. Fouled screws frequently resulted in broaching unless a salvage vessel or boat was immediately available to handle the situation.

LVT's

LVT(A)'s led the assault and supported the landing by fire on the objective beaches. LVT's landed the assault troops as scheduled in the Landing Attack Order and were thereafter used in landing cargo. LVT(A)'s continued to support the assault by covering the flanks of the beaches, by close-in fire from the water against caves and other prepared positions close to the shore and by furnishing support to troop units holding lines extending to the water. No attempt was made to take them far inland or to use them as tanks due to their vulnerability when not waterborne.

LVT's were particularly useful in this operation due to the difficulties encountered in operating wheeled vehicles in the soft sand of the beaches. They were used in unloading from the LST's during the early stages of the assault and moved their loads to inland dumps or to provide direct troop support.

Conditions were not favorable for LVT operation as there was at all times sufficient swell to make handling in and out of LST's a difficult matter. Sea and surf conditions were such that any overloading of LVT's was liable to result in swamping. They are not good heavy weather craft; when loaded, freeboard may be reduced to a point where more water is shipped than hand pumps can handle. In case of engine failure LVT's must be taken on board LST's or towed to the beach promptly; otherwise, there is positive danger of sinking. Although the inadequacy of emergency hand operated pumps has been stated in every report of operations, no action to overcome this defect has yet been taken.

The operation of LVT's is primarily the responsibility of the LVT battalion officers. To better enable these officers to supervise LVT operation, provision has been made for their assignment to control vessels stationed off the various beaches in order that they may exercise more direct control. When swells are heavy or the sea becomes rough, it may be impossible to reembark LVT's in LST's either for security, loading, or servicing. When LVT operations continue day and night it is necessary that LVT's know locations of the LST's which they are unloading. LVT's have limited visibility and indifferent sea keeping qualities. Although primary responsibility for LVT operation may rest with the battalion officers, commanding officers of LST's working with or servicing LVT's control officers and beachmasters likewise have very definite responsibilities for the continued and effective operation of LVT's as follows:

LST COMMANDING OFFICERS

Advise the control officer, and through him the beachmaster of the beach off which he is operating, whenever he is required to leave his assigned station or is unable to maintain it.

Advise officers directing LVT operations if, for any reason, he is unable to take LVT's on board either for salvage, servicing, or unloading.

An LST commanding officer shall assist any LVT which is in trouble to the best of his ability. If he is unable to take the LVT on board for repairs and service, he shall immediately advise the control officer of the nearest beach or himself take steps for its salvage.

DUKW'S

Difficulty was likewise experienced in handling DUKW's on the soft sand beaches. DUKW tires, even when deflated, had a tendency to dig into the sand causing the DUKW to belly. It was usually necessary to tow them clear of the beach, using tractors, until beach matting had been laid or ramps built to the water's edge. On occasion, experienced drivers were unable to negotiate the beaches by putting the vehicle in low gear, deflating tires, and making a slow approach. Many DUKW's were broached; however, a large percentage of them were later salvaged.

As sea and surf conditions became worse, the operation of DUKW's became increasingly difficult. As in the case of LVT's, it is not possible to embark DUKW's in a rough sea with a heavy swell. If the DUKW is loaded, the difficulties of embarkation are increased. In many instances DUKW's were loaded and sent to the beach when surf conditions were such that DUKW's could not land without serious danger of swamping and broaching. Their recovery by the parent LST was also impracticable. The result was that a number of loaded DUKW's which could neither land nor be reembarked were held off the beaches. As in the case of the LVT, hand pumps were inadequate. The result was that DUKW's which had engine failures or which ran out of gas and were not promptly refueled, sank off the beaches. There was a general tendency to overload these vehicles based on theoretical capacities. A safe load for a DUKW under average operating conditions is about 5,000 pounds, the normal load of an LCVP. Operating conditions off Iwo Jima were not good; however, many DUKW's were loaded with cargo in excess of 7,000 pounds in spite of DUKW company officers' recommendations to the contrary. These craft usually were the first to swamp, thus losing both vehicle and load.

Many of the remarks which have been made in connection with the operation of LVT's are equally applicable to the operation of DUKW's. The officers of the DUKW companies should exercise close control over their vehicles. LST's assigned to servicing DUKW's and which are being unloaded by DUKW's must keep the officers of the DUKW companies informed as to their movements and their ability to recover vehicles. The launching of DUKW's should be controlled by an officer who knows their capabilities; they should not be launched if they cannot land. LST commanding officers, control officers, and beachmasters have responsibilities for DUKW operation similar to those with which they are charged for LVT operation.

In future operations DUKW company officers should ride the control vessels stationed off the beaches to which DUKW's are unloading. It is necessary that all available information be passed to those officers, both afloat and ashore, who are responsible for the successful employment of these vehicles in unloading.

WEASELS

The Weasel is only semiamphibious; its low freeboard and resulting light load capacity would prevent it from being used as a ship-to-shore cargo carrier under any but ideal conditions. However, it is able to negotiate almost any kind of terrain and can carry loads up to about 500 pounds. It is believed that there are distinct possibilities for the employment of this vehicle over flat coral reefs in shallow water where swamping is unlikely and its speed, maneuverability, and ability to surmount abrupt slopes may make it invaluable, although its primary function may not be that of hauling cargo. Conditions may be readily visualized under which it will be the only satisfactory vehicle available for unloading.

From: *Commanding General Expeditionary Troops (CTF–56)*

The value of this vehicle (Weasel) cannot be overemphasized. During the early phases of the assault, they were used extensively and proved invaluable in supplying front line troops with medical supplies and ammunition.

From: *Commander Amphibious Forces, United States Pacific Fleet (Commander Joint Expeditionary Force)*

BARGES AND CAUSEWAYS

The steep beaches and heavy surf made it impossible to use the barges for unloading purposes. The only barges which were satisfactorily employed as intended were those used in connec tion with the casualty evacuation LST's. These barges, four in number, were moored alongside the LST's, and since they rose and fell with the sea together with the small craft carrying casualties from the beach, enabled quick unloading of the small craft and rapid transfer of casualties to the LST's. It is estimated that many lives were saved due to the rapid transfer of casualties effected by the use of barges.

The nature of the beach and surf made construction of piers and causeways impracticable. Attempts to construct piers only resulted in the pontoon sections broaching on the beach, damaging other craft and obstructing the beach. The only useful accomplishment of the causeways was the construction of a 4 by 30 fuel barge from causeways carried on LST *761*. This was anchored off Yellow 1 and in use throughout the assault.

LST(M)

The Iwo Jima operation marked the first appearance of a new type of logistic vessel, the LST Landing Craft Tender, familiarly known as the "mother ship." Of the four LST's converted to LST(M)'s as a result of experience gained in the Marianas campaign, two took part in the Iwo Jima operation. They were constructed with 20 "reefer" boxes in the tank deck for carrying 160,000 rations of fresh and frozen provisions, stowage space for 160,000 rations of dry provisions, bunks for 350 additional enlisted men in the tank deck, bunks for 40 officers in a quonset hut on the main deck, an extra galley also housed in a main deck quonset hut, additional washroom facilities, and large evaporators. These ships were designed to act both as a "home" for transients and boat crews left behind at the objective upon nightly retirement of transports, and as supply ships for small craft ranging from PCEs through LCTs.

In this function they were eminently successful, berthing a total of over 2,500 officers and men, subsisting 4,900 officers and men, refueling and watering 54 vessels and reprovisioning 76 vessels, all between D-day and D-plus-15. Their value should be even greater during a longer operation, where the prospect of a hot meal, a shower and a good night's sleep for "stray" boat crews, and fresh provisions for the small craft, will doubtless serve as an excellent morale builder.

From: Commander Task Group 53.4 (Commander LSM Flotilla 5)

Damage from loading alongside transports constituted an estimated 93 percent of all damage sustained. As a whole it may be classed as serious, and for the most part unavoidable, since not only bad or poor weather contributed to the damage, but also the inherent design features of all LSM's lead to the inevitable damaging of every port side of every vessel including title A, B, and C equipment there installed. Again it is pointed out that this is a general report; consequently, the following information is in no way specific but presented only as an over-all picture of damage incurred while alongside transports loading.

In future operations APA's and AKA's must provide suitable fenders to prevent damage to themselves and LSM's while alongside. Fenders should be at least 15 feet in length, made of telephone poles lashed three together to distribute the pressure over a large area.

LIFE SAVING DEVICES

From: Commander Task Group 58.2 (Commander Carrier Division 2)

An excellent measure adopted by *Franklin* was that of securing metal Jacob's ladders at various points around the elevated parts of the ship including the island structure. The top of these ladders were shackled into welded eyes. Manila life lines are not satisfactory because they burn away and are too difficult to ascend and descend.

The kapok life jacket proved superior to the pneumatic lifebelt in two important respects. First it provides splinter protection to the man who wears it, and, second, it gives better support in the water. Topside personnel should be required to wear life jackets at all times when air attack is probable. Many personnel who were not wearing life jackets were blown over the side from *Franklin*. Additional spare life jackets should be stowed in quantity on the forecastle and stern, the two most probable gathering places for personnel prior to abandoning ship.

Life jackets fitted with slabs of Doron, a fibrous spun glass material ⅛-inch thick, are being issued to the amphibious forces. This body armor, weighing 8 pounds, will stop a .45-caliber bullet and a high percentage of fragments. It covers a man's trunk and abdomen and thus protects those parts where most of the fatal wounds occur. To date 300,000 life jackets so fitted have been sent to the operating areas.

SMOKE

From: *Commander Amphibious Group Two* (*CTF 53 and CTG 51.21*)

Smoke again proved to be invaluable as protective cover for ships in the transport area against detection by enemy planes during night air raids. Enemy planes flew over the smoke hidden ships apparently unable to take any effective action. Smoke was used 16 times for a total of 9 hours and 47 minutes. During these raids no ships in the smoke screen were hit by bombs. The U. S. S. *Auburn* (AGC 10), completely covered with smoke, was straddled by five bombs with the closest one landing approximately 300 yards away. Smoke was not used in the daytime to cover transports.

Very little difficulty was encountered with the operation of the portable oil fog generators. Their performance throughout the operation was most satisfying. These generators are capable of emitting large volumes of nontoxic smoke that persists for long distances downwind. No trouble was encountered by Floating Smoke Pots M4A2 and Mk3 pots igniting spontaneously. The floating smoke pots are invaluable for establishing a quick screen and maintaining it at the source.

From: *Commander Amphibious Forces, United States Pacific Fleet* (*Commander Joint Expeditionary Force*)

The plan for covering the transport area with smoke during air attacks consisted basically of stationing LCI type vessels and other small craft equipped with Besler (or Todd) fog generators in a line across the windward side of the transport area. In addition, each transport in the area stationed two LCVP's, equipped with light weight fog generator (or smoke pots) and smoke floats to windward of the parent vessel. The transports also made smoke, utilizing fog generators installed on board.

Ships and boats were ordered to commence smoking when "bogeys" were observed on the radar screen in such a position and on such a course that an air attack seemed likely. The use of smoke more or less paralleled "Flash Red."

Smoke was not used during daylight as protection against enemy aircraft.

While at Saipan en route to Iwo Jima the Transport Area Smoke Plan was executed during the afternoon to test its effectiveness during daylight. The conclusion was that the advantages obtained from smoke during daylight air attacks are outweighed by the disadvantage of reducing effectiveness of gunfire.

From: *Commanding Officer U. S. S. "Salt Lake City"* (*CA*)

FS smoke is decidedly irritating to the respiratory system, and should not be used in any position where the wind blows it over the gun stations. It completely ruins the efficiency of the gun crews. One gun crew thus exposed during an enemy air raid was sent to the sickbay for examination and four had enough respiratory disturbance to require absolute rest for 24 hours. All of this group were required to bathe immediately using considerable soap and water to relieve the burning sensation experienced in the exposed skin. It is believed a sulfurous acid is formed on contact with moist surfaces. Evidences of its activity on bits and shields about the stern were also noted.

GROUND WEAPONS

From: *Commanding General, Headquarters Fourth Marine Division, Fleet Marine Force*

Comment.—Experience gained in the Iwo Jima operation emphasized the need for a heavier and more powerful direct fire weapon than the Bazooka for use of assault teams against concrete emplacements and caves, employing a shell with concrete-piercing capabilities against the former and a fragmentation shell for attack of the latter.

Recommendation.—That a short range rocket of 4.5" caliber, capable of being crew served by two men of the assault team and firing concrete-piercing and fragmentation ammunition, be adopted.

Comment.—The need for additional mortars in the division, particularly a heavier type mortar than the 81-mm., was apparent in the operation. Heavier mortars should be employed to supplement the organic 81-mm. mortar platoons and provide the infantry commander with vitally needed additional fire support to bridge the gap between the 81 mm. and artillery.

Recommendation.—That the 4″2 mortar be adopted by the Marine Corps and a mortar battalion of two 4″2 companies and one 155-mm. mortar company be assigned to each division.

Captured 155-mm. Mortar With Bipod Attached.

Rugged Terrain in the Northern Part of the Island Made Progress Difficult and Casualties High.

Entrance to Japanese 81-mm. Mortar Ammunition Dump.

Rugged Terrain in the Northern Part of the Island Made Progress Difficult and Casualties High.

* 9 7 8 1 7 8 0 3 9 5 0 4 3 *